The Perfect Cast

Publisher's Note

This anthology contains extracts from works from many different periods. To maintain the original feel of the writing we have kept to the author's original style as published instead of standardising the text. In the American extracts American spellings have been retained.

The Perfect Cast

A Celebration of Fly-fishing

Edited by Tom Quinn

Quiller

Compilation copyright © 2011 Quiller Publishing Ltd

First published in the UK in 2011
by Quiller, an imprint of Quiller Publishing Ltd

British Library Cataloguing-in-Publication Data
A catalogue record for this book
is available from the British Library

ISBN 978 1 84689 042 0

Jacket and book design by Sharyn Troughton

Printed in China

Quiller

An imprint of Quiller Publishing Ltd
Wykey House, Wykey, Shrewsbury, SY4 1JA
Tel: 01939 261616 Fax: 01939 261606
E-mail: info@quillerbooks.com
Website: www.countrybooksdirect.com

Contents

Credits

The author and publishers are grateful to the following for permission to reproduce copyright material in this book:

Nick Lyons' *Spring Creeks* first published in 1992 by Atlantic Monthly Press

Dave Hughes' *Trout from Small Streams* excerpt first published in 2002 by Stackpole Books

Paul Schullery's *The Rise* excerpt first published in 2006 by Stackpole Books

Ed Engle's *Fishing Small Flies* excerpt first published in 2005 by Stackpole Books

Eldridge Hardie's painting from *The Paintings of Eldridge Hardie* first published in 2002 by Stackpole Books

Dave Hall's painting *On the Way*

Tom Rosenbauer *The Seven-Cigar Trout*

James R. Babb *Fishing the Flats*

Where possible artists and photographers are named in captions and every effort has been made by the editor to trace copyright holders. If there are any omissions he will be happy to include these in future editions.

Acknowledgements

Thanks to all those whose stories, pictures and sculpture are included here, and to Charlotte, Alex, James, Katy and Joe. Thanks also to John Beaton, Rob Dixon, Carolyn Longbottom, Judith Schnell and Amy Lerner.

Introduction

Fly-fishing is a difficult art to master. If we just wanted to catch fish we would use a worm or a net and that would be the end of it. But fly-fishing puts the fish on the bank in the most challenging way possible, using a delicate creation of fur, feather and tinsel; a creation that, in many instances, attempts precisely to mimic a real fly.

Thousands of highly imaginative and sometimes extraordinary fly patterns have been created over the years, not to mention ever more sophisticated techniques for using them. Fly-fishing is, in short, a highly creative business.

And if creativity lies at the heart of fly fishing then it is perhaps no great surprise that those who fish have always enjoyed the literature of fishing as well as paintings, drawings and sculpture that try to capture, for a moment at least, the essence of this most compelling pastime.

This book attempts to bring together the best and most interesting art and literature associated with fly-fishing from more than four centuries. I have included artists old and new from both sides of the Atlantic together with extracts from books both well known and, in some cases, entirely forgotten.

The extracts cover fly-fishing for salmon, trout and sea trout from river, lake and stream. They also include tales of extraordinary events, of famous anglers and eccentrics, of great days on famous rivers, and, of course, of beautiful places. Inevitably there are tales of the one that got away together with stories that confirm the old suspicion that some anglers are very lucky indeed.

But whatever your interest, whether salmon, trout or sea trout, you will find something here to conjure again those magical days by the water's edge and to remind you that fly-fishing is indeed about far more than catching fish.

Verse and Worse

Go softly by that river-side, or when you would depart,
You'll find its every winding tied, and knotted round your heart.

Rudyard Kipling

Dedication

It costs so little to dream a while
Almost nothing per thousand mile;
A pauper can go through Gretna Green
To Ballachulish or Achnasheen
Or travel the road round dour loch Eil
And sort his flies on the Bridge of Shiel

It costs so little to cast a fly
In dreamland where the curlews cry
To smell bog-myrtle and burning peat
Where the rushing burns and a lochan meet.

George Brennand

Little Blew Dun

Made of the down of a mouse for body and head, dubt with sad, ash-coloured silk, wing of the sad coloured feather of a sheepstare quill.

James Chetham, *The Anglers' Vade Mecum*, 1681

Pilgrimage

When in my pilgrimage I reach
The river that we all must cross
And land upon that further beach
Where earthly gains are counted loss

May I not earthly loss repair?
Well if those fish should rise again,
There shall be no more parting there –
Celestial gut will stand the strain.

And issuing from the portal one
Who was himself a fisherman,
Will drop his keys and shouting run
To help me land Leviathan.

Colin Ellis

The Trout

Should you lure,

From his dark haunt, beneath the tangled roots

Of pendant trees, the monarch of the brook,

Behoves you then to ply your finest art.

Long time he, following, cautious scans the fly,

And oft attempts to seize it, but as oft

The dimpled water speaks his jealous fear.

At last while haply o'er the shaded sun

Passes a cloud, he desperate takes the bait

With sullen plunge; at once he darts along

Deep struck and runs out all the lengthn'd line,

Then seeks the farthest ooze, the sheltering weed,

The cavern'd bank, his old secure abode,

And flies aloft, and flounces round the pool,

Indignant of the guile.

James Thompson, from *The Seasons*, 1730

Fly-fishing: The Magic

The Red Hole

A few hundred yards above the Durngate Mill and at no great distance below the city bathing place in the north-east corner of the park, the western stream of the Abbots Barton water divides into two streams, about half the current passing through two brick arches into a round deepish pool a nice cast across, then turning and running under a bridge of planking – to follow parallel the part that bounds the park and to be known as Swift Lake. Swift Lake seldom contains a sizeable trout, yet Red Hole, as the round pool below the brick arches is known, has yielded me and my friends and guests many a sturdy trout, rarely scaling less than 2 lb.

It was from the upper brick arch that 'Wary Willie', whose passing was described in *Minor Tactics of the Chalk Stream*, was extracted, but he was caught from the park side (the west) of the side stream before the park ground was acquired by Winchester and made into a park. The pool known as the Red Hole seldom showed a trout much further than a couple of yards below the two brick arches and Swift Lake seldom showed a trout at all – yet the Red Hole was always worth a few casts close up to one or other of the brick arches, preferably the northern one.

At one time, and one only, do I recall a good trout lying for two successive weekends in Swift Lake, a yard or two below the planking bridge, and, not realising that he was there or even suspecting that

a sizeable fish might be there, I put him down. At the following weekend I had as my guest an officer who had the V.C. after his name, for some feat of gallantry on the Afghan frontiers, and I had provided him with a Leonard rod, carrying a No. 3 line dressed by N.D. Coggeshall. We crossed the lower side stream from the park by a boat from the south-east corner, and walked up between the stream we had crossed and Swift Lake till near the planking, when I told my guest of the trout I had seen and recommended him to wait and, if the fish were there and rose, to offer him the home-made red sedge which I provided. The fish was there and took the fly at

Mayfly time by Richard Smith

the first offer – but was missed in the strike. He was, however, so little alarmed that before many minutes he rose again. My guest was about to cast, but I recommended a change of fly as the fish had had reason to suspect the red sedge as a 'wrong un' and he was in a place where there was no regular hatch, and I tied on a Tup's Indispensable. A few minutes later I had the satisfaction of netting out for my guest a nice stout fish of 2 lb 3 oz.

Another guest of mine whom I led to the Red Hole was the famous Dr Francis Ward. Him also I provided with a little red sedge – and I saved him from a smash, possibly involving rod top, at the planking bridge, by telling him how to turn his fish and keep it in the pool when it was mad to get away under the plank bridge. That was another two-pounder. Dr Francis Ward came again on several occasions and seldom failed to visit the Red Hole and get a two-pounder.

Whether I entered the meadows at Durngate Mill or at the park corner, by boat I seldom omitted to cast a red sedge at the brick arches, and I cannot say how many two-pounders were extracted by my friends – Dr Norman McCaskie of Green Cat fame and others – from that marvellous Red Hole.

One never saw the trout lying below the brick arches – but if one kept on casting for a while there was often a response sooner or later. I remember one evening when Dr McCaskie and I came up together along Swift Lake and he gave up after casting fifteen or twenty minutes at the Red Hole. Within five minutes of his leaving disappointed for the main river I was busy playing a 2 lb 6 oz trout.

I remember leaving a riser just above the cottage by Winnal St Magdalen to rest him, going to the Red Hole and getting a two-pounder and offering the same red sedge on my return to the trout I had rested, and taking it with a dash. I made no secret of the spot – but none of the other members of the syndicate ever made much of it. I suspect the reason was the little red sedge.

G.E.M. Skues, *Itchen Memories*, 1951

He's on! Autumn fishing by Ernest Briggs

The Right Fly

However easily scared a trout may be when he is not feeding, he is bold to indifference when he is. Thus when the fish are rising you may hook, play, land, and kill a dozen fish without moving from the spot on which you stand.

I have often done so, and the other day had a good opportunity of seeing what occurs under these circumstances. I was fishing the Bourne in Hampshire; and throwing at one of two fish which were busily feeding within a yard of each other. At last I hooked him and we had a battle – he to get under a bush, in the shadow of which the second one was feeding, and I to keep him out. The result was that the hubbub about and around the second fish was very great, yet he never moved, and as soon as I landed my friend and the current was restored number two went on feeding, and I believe if I could have got a fly over him (which I could not on account of the bush) I should have killed both fish.

When trout are on the feed and have risen at and not taken your fly, they will seldom come again (a grayling will, but a trout as a rule will not); he has to all appearance made up his mind that the lure is a wrong one. But at the right fly he certainly will come twice, and that even after he has been hooked. Fishing in the Test at Laverstock last summer, after changing my fly several times over a large trout which was actively feeding under the opposite bank, I put on a little yellow one and hooked him, and then, after a good struggle against stream, when just pulling him in the net – he got off. 'Why, sir,' said the keeper, 'he has gone back again and is feeding again.'

'So he is, and in the same spot too. But you will see he will not look at it again,' and out went the fly, just to see what he would do. To the astonishment of both of us he took it, and to his own, no doubt, when he found himself engaged in a second struggle for his life all within the space of five minutes, and this time in vain, for he was soon in my basket. On the same stream, and only a few days previously, the keeper saw Sir Maurice Duff-Gordon (a first-rate fisherman) lose a fish by his line breaking, and on the same afternoon with a similar fly catch him – the first hook being well-embedded in his tongue. So much for the sensibility of fish, and for their not coming a second time at the fly they approve of.

This is not at all an unfrequent occurrence and must happen to all fly fishers. Last spring I lost a fine fish in the Chess. He had taken the Red Spinner, got into the weeds, and broke me. In the afternoon I saw a fish rising at the same spot; threw the Red Spinner over him, and had him at once. He weighed over two pounds, and had my morning fly in his upper jaw.

Edward Hamilton, *Fly Fishing,* 1884

Chalkstream fishing at mayfly time photograph by John Tarlton

Saving a Blank

It was as cold a May day as I remember. The sky was a dirty grey, a wild gusty wind blew from the north, and the young green of the trees seemed to have lost all freshness and brilliance. The Test ran swift and full, but even its clear water looked dark, dull and forbidding.

Not a fish showed till two o'clock. The morning passed without a sign of life, and the weather if anything grew worse. I ate my sandwiches walking, to keep warm. At last a fish did actually rise, but it must have been due entirely to light-heartedness, for there was nothing to rise at. However, he took a blue upright ribbed with gold wire and proved on landing to be nearly two pounds in weight. An unenterprising animal: but I was cheered to get him. Time was running, and it was something to save a blank, for assuredly no day ever looked more like a blank. After landing him, I began to walk upstream. Only one other rod was out, he was far below me, and there were four empty beats above mine. Better move towards home, thought I: perhaps things may be more prosperous above: anyhow nothing is lost thereby, there is good fishing all the way. So up I walked slowly, watching the water like a hawk. Three o'clock came; the gale was more violent than ever, and colder. Even my optimism began to desert me. And then, unexpectedly, things began to happen.

I forget what it was that first attracted my attention, probably the splash of a fish, for the water was whipped into such waves that flies and even rises were hard to see. At all events, I suddenly realised that the river, as if by magic, was speckled with iron blues. Blown sideways by the gusts, hurried downstream by the wild wind, children of the storm that they are, on they came, their narrow purple wings looking too delicate to live out the gale, ever more and more of them, till every square foot of the surface carried them. And, equally suddenly, trout began rising, good trout, and rising strongly and well, as they always do in a downstream wind.

All this takes longer to tell than it did to experience. I crept up to a rising fish, knelt down, and began lengthening my line. Oh that wind! It was not even dead in my face, it was right into my shoulder, the hardest of all against which to throw. But the first cast that went near my fish he took, and rushed madly downstream, my reel screaming. I had to take him a long way before I got him out, a beauty of 2 lb 2 oz. That was better. A brace.

I walked quickly back to where I had hooked him, and looked up. Then I saw that provided I made no mess of it, I might do great things. Just above me was a pool, very deep, with a swift turbulent stream coming in at right angles at the head and a quicker run also at right angles below. You know the sort of pool: full of swirls, eddies, and cross currents, inhabited by large and experienced trout, who roam about, now rising in the backwater, now in the current, then moving into almost still water, and eating half a dozen nearly stationary flies. On a calm day, you can catch them, if you see or guess which way they are turning, and drop your fly almost on their nose, putting it right into their mouths. But to do this you must cast very accurately, you must be at the top of your form. Moreover, you must cast very often: for owing to the different currents running in all directions, your fly will only float an inch or two without drag: and before it drags you must whip it off and cast again: for cunning trout must never see drag, never, never. All this constant casting is very tiring, even when all is in your favour, on a calm day. It is much more so with a wind against you, for accurate placing is infinitely harder, and you have to take three or four throws to do what you should do in one.

So difficult did it seem that I halted a moment, in quick indecision. Should I tackle this water, holding big trout, but horribly difficult in a head wind, or should I move on to the even-flowing beat above? The question was settled for me. A fish rose just where the quick run left the pool, on the very lip, and if ever I saw a fish between 3 lb and 4 lb it was he. No fisherman could possibly leave such a prize. After several bad shots, I got the fly in front of him; he rose confidently, I struck, but too quickly, and missed him. I waited, cursing myself: but after a minute, yes, there he was rising again, rising again regularly. I had not pricked him. I nipped off my blue upright and knotted on a winged iron blue. This floated beautifully over him. He rose again, and this time he was hooked. He made one bolt up into the pool, jumped, then turned and rushed down the racing stream below. I ran back into the meadow to keep the line taut, but he came so fast that it got slack. I reeled furiously, felt the fish, off he careered again, but my line brushed against something, underwater weed no doubt; only a touch, but it was enough, he was off. What a tragedy.

It was no use lamenting. Mechanically I took off the iron blue, and tied on a blue upright again. I walked back to where I had hooked him. Fly was thicker than ever, chiefly iron blue, but also large winter duns, small dark olives and medium olives, a wonderful sight, only to be seen on a chalk stream. Something

moved far over the river. The throw, being across the wind, was easier, but I laid the fly down too hard and it sank. He took it all the same. I pulled, and felt fast as a rock. He also dashed downstream, but I could keep the line tight, I ran down and got below him on a short line, and we fought out a desperate battle over 200 yards of water. A lovely trout, 3 lb 7 oz, a picture to look at.

But I wasted no time admiring him. Several were rising in the swirly water, and would undoubtedly take if I could get a fly to them. It was hard work to do this, and tiring, too, in that bitter wind: for with roaming fish you may put the fly off their tail instead of before their nose, many casts are needed even on a calm day, and even more on such a storm-swept water. I failed at three fish running, owing to drag and wind, thoroughly rousing their suspicions, but doing nothing more. Then I got one, well over the pound and a half limit. By that time, all the fish in that particular pool had been either caught, risen, or frightened. It was possible, no doubt, to get another, or more than one: but that involved giving the pool a rest, and time was running. So I reeled in, and walked quickly up to the beat above. Here the broad shining Test ran straight, with a swift, even current and the problem would be easier. The fish, too, had had a mighty meal undisturbed, and at the same time had not had time to eat too much, and grow dainty and suspicious. But what was even better, the wind had fallen perceptibly. The fly still floated down steadily, less thick certainly, but in quite sufficient quantity.

The first trout I spotted was rising close under my bank. A left-handed cast, straight into the wind he was, and many were the throws I made before my fly, an iron blue this time, went right. He was lying above some tall dead grasses, and the shot had to be accurate, or the line bounced off the grass, and the fly blew wide. But at last he had it, and when struck bolted across the river, my rod bending double. I worked him down, and had my net off the sling to net him, when all unexpectedly the fly came away. My next fish also escaped. When hooked, he rushed across the river in a succession of jumps, falling back into the water with a smash, and at the last leap he threw the hook. Both were heavy fish. Such things will happen. Next I wasted precious minutes over a fish

which when landed proved to be just undersized, and I began to get anxious. The fly was growing scarcer, and the day was drawing in. After such a hatch, was I to return with only four trout? I walked slowly up, scanning the water. At last, there he is, right under the opposite bank, and a beauty too, for I can see him. In some ways, the cross-stream cast is the easiest, for if you are cunning and throw six inches short, the trout never sees your gut and will turn his head out to take your fly. And so it happened. I waited till he had turned back, and gave a good pull. It was long before this gallant fish yielded, but he did so at last. He weighed only one ounce under three pounds. And just as I got him out another fish put up his head in midstream, and he too was caught. I looked at my watch. It was six o'clock and all was over. I had bagged six fish, and under their comfortable weight I trudged happily homewards.

Now what, I said to myself, were the particular features of that admirable day? First of all, the hatch of fly. It is nearly forty years since I caught my first trout on the Test, and it is the fashion to say that the fly then was much more plentiful than now. This was undoubtedly true even five years ago: whether it is true now I feel doubtful. Certainly mayfly is very thick again, and not only mayfly, for I am sure that the small fly is increasing too. Indeed, I have rarely seen a greater hatch. True, it did not last long, about three hours: but during the time it was on the river was covered. They are very wonderful things, these big hatches, one of the great events of nature. Oh, the Test is not decadent, I said to myself, it is still the greatest of trout streams. Next the weather. Most writers upon chalk streams tell us about sun and flowers and summer meadows. The iron blue loves none of these. He delights in rough and bitter winds, grey skies, and cold air. He rejoices in our hard northern spring. And the more he is buffeted, the more happily he rides out the storm. Lastly, when the iron blue is on, trout prefer it to any other fly. On this day there had been quantities of insects, amongst them that favourite food, the winter dun; yet I saw nothing eaten except the iron blue.

Thus ended the day, a day of hard work, and of failure mingled with success. What more can the fisherman desire? And what sport can compare with fishing?

J.W. Hills, *A Summer on the Test*, 1924

Salmon leaping, drypoint etching by Norman Wilkinson

A Lost Fish Enjoyed

Perhaps it is a form of masochism born of incipient senility, but I have come to believe that I actually enjoy losing fish.

When very small, I made a spectacular start on my fish-losing career. The senior members of the family were fishing in Loch Mudle from the safe comfort of a boat; I had been dismissed to the burn.

Suddenly a swirl like a seal at play sent my heart plunging through my stomach. I struck wildly, and a great fish steamed down the swollen burn with small boy in pursuit. At the age of eight I had no clear standard of comparison, but I knew this was no ordinary burn sea trout. With helpless desperation I hung on while the salmon did what it liked.

Fortunately, there were no trees along the bank, no waterfalls or rapids, and I was able to prevent him taking out all the line by running after him. How that fish didn't break me I shall never know: but after what seemed an eternity, it lay below me, tired and almost motionless, within reach of my net. The burn was deep, and the heather hung far out over the bank. The net was tiny, little more than a toy. It was all I could do to reach the giant fish at full stretch without falling through the heather into 6 ft of water.

He was too big for the net, but I did get his tail end in, and for a moment he was balanced in mid air on his way to the bank. But his unexpected weight, once out of the water, was too much for me. The net wobbled, he gave a last flop, and I saw – and even heard – the gut snap just above the fly.

He lay there stunned for a second, and I could see the gleam of the Mallard and Silver in his upper jaw. Without waiting to think, splash! I threw down rod and net and jumped straight on top of him. The water was well out of my depth but that didn't matter, because I felt him in my arms for a fraction of a second before he escaped with a wriggle and a flap. That feeling will be with me to my dying day. As I kicked my way to the surface I saw a great wave as he sped through the shallows at the head of the pool, and away…

No-one but a born fisherman can understand the agony of that moment. I wept, and for years afterwards the pain returned whenever I thought of it. There had been no witnesses; the memory had to remain an unshared secret. Over the years, I have lost a great many more fish. Habit has dulled the pain. Grown-ups don't weep. 'I accept the universe!' said some gushing lady to Thomas Carlyle. 'Gad! You'd better!' was his sardonic reply. These words have inspired me to look back at all the fish I've lost in a new way. How much happier a place the world must be for all those prize trout still at large! One remembers all the fish one loses,

Gallant fighter. scraperboard by Denys Watkins Pitchford

not many of those one catches. How rich in such memories I have become! While others point to desiccated specimens of such and such a weight, caught in such and such a place on a given date, growing dusty in glass cases on the unlit side of the front hall, mine lurk alive and still growing, monstrous shadowy forms forever haunting the deep waters of my vivid memory.

Now, like many middle-aged fishermen, I've philosophised my way to an almost oriental patient-at-oneness with the will of the wind and the waters. When I first took my sons down to the Tweed, my heart beat wildly to see the primeval emotions flitting across their faces – as failure and success followed one another in their eternally unjust and erratic way. I have to recognise that my

role is now that of the elder statesman, counselling patience and calm in every adversity. I've fished that water for thirty years; I've hooked and lost salmon on my trout rod. It has nothing worse in store, no new horror to sear my battle-scarred soul.

On the Saturday of the Melrose seven-a-sides, which I should have been watching, I went down to Lord Haig's stretch with my son, Bede. It is lovely water with a stately salmon pool below a wooded bank spattered with primroses. Up and downstream, the broad Tweed curves its way at the bottom of a 300 ft valley with sides which defy access. How beautiful the April waters on this sparkling day, and how misleading. The wading is difficult and treacherous at the Gate Heugh above 400 yards of tumbling trout runs.

In low water the depth varies from 1½ to 3 ft with a narrow channel for the mainstream some 3 ft deeper; an ideal succession of half-pools and half-rapids. Given a heavy shower, the river rises rapidly by a further dangerous 2 ft. The bottom consists of a blend of large slippery boulders and shelving rocks, which can plunge one over the top of one's waders into the powerful current at any time. We fished our way up this formidable stretch with toil and tribulation. Few trout were showing, although we had seen an 11 lb salmon landed. I had two small trout and a grayling, and Bede, cold and wet after two blank and unlucky days, was on the point of giving up in despair.

At the top of the Gate Heugh is a big flat rock; casting upstream from it, I have caught many a good trout, including my best-ever Tweed brown trout of 1 lb 14 oz. Cold and tired, I had just concluded that no more trout would be rising for it was past three o'clock. Nevertheless, the rock offered comparative comfort, and I continued for a few moments, and was encouraged by rising and missing a good fish. There was a promising-looking eddy a little further out, so I ventured out from the rock into the deeper water, and on a long line rose and this time hooked another. To my surprise it tore my line out upstream in the irresistible way which announces something really substantial. Instead of stopping after the first surge, it went on. I held on nervously as my little 8 ft rod bent alarmingly, and remembered that it was last year's nylon, and 4 lb breaking strain at that. What sort of hold had my tiny Greenwell got? The fish leaped, silhouetted against the dancing, dazzling sunlit ripples. It was big, but I couldn't see it clearly, it looked too dark for a grilse or a sea trout.

There followed a grim battle as the fish swung round me in a semi-circle, boring deep. I tried to recover line, and it came to within a few feet. I fumbled at my net, but my best efforts to hold against the current failed, and it took out more line, until it was far below me, and I wondered whether I could ever stop it. For a long time there was deadlock, but eventually I got some line back and saw him come up to the surface with a great back fin. Clearly he was a brown trout, but I could not guess the size except to say

that he was certainly over 4 lb, and the hardest-fighting trout I had ever felt.

I brought him almost within netting range again, but he was plainly just resting, for he swirled to the top, jumped again, making my rod rattle, and made off downstream like a marlin. By this time, Bede, who had seen the fight from far below, was struggling up to see the fun. Despairing of ever forcing the fish up against the current and not daring to make for the bank, because the perilous wading might make me stumble and fall, I remained uneasily perched on top of a vast submarine boulder, praying I should not lose my balance. Slowly I coaxed him round to the inshore side of me, hoping that Bede, 20 yds below me, might be able to net him in the quieter and shallower waters.

I had always believed there were giant trout in the Gate Heugh and now I would be able to prove it. I briefly visualised whether this one would look better in a glass case in the entrance hall or the drawing room. But now the devil must have entered into him, for suddenly, he was away again. His strength took me aback, the rod bent to a croquet hoop as the fish made straight for Bede, who wisely resisted having a dab with the net as the line actually brushed against his waders.

I nearly lost my foothold, got my balance again and tried to slow the fish, only to be encountered by a final burst of power – and he was away! The fly had gone with him and the line flapped loose. All philosophy forgotten, I swore and bellowed, and even thrashed the river with my impotent and fly-less cast, like John Cleese thrashing his car for stalling. In my fury I actually jumped up and down like a naughty child, staggered, slipped over the top of my waders, and wrenched my arm in my attempt to recover. All the accumulated misery of every fish ever lost came back multiplied a hundred-fold as I cursed the river, the sport and the futility of life.

With a final bellow of pain and anger, I looked towards my son for sympathy.

He was roaring with laughter.

Logie Bruce Lockhart, *The Pleasures of Fishing*, 1981

On the Rise

The rise of a trout is far from being the only thing that matters about fly fishing, but it is for many of us the most exciting thing. As a thrilling act of predation and an exhilarating affirmation or devastating condemnation of our streamcraft, the rise is at the center of the small universe of interests, crafts, and passions that make up the sport. I'm far from the first to notice that all the other parts of fly fishing revolve, sometimes quite erratically and distantly, around that one crucial moment when a fish decides to feed.

It is both odd and wonderful that up until that instant, though we may have put immense amounts of time, thought, and energy into getting there, the trout has been without concern for us and our ways. The trout's wildness and independence are what make each cast so important to us.

In *A Sand County Almanac* (1949), the visionary ecologist-conservationist Aldo Leopold told of a brief 'fishing idyl' on a Wisconsin trout stream. For a few minutes, he sat and considered 'the ways of trout and men'.

How like fish we are: ready, nay eager, to seize upon whatever new thing some wind of circumstance shakes down upon the river of time. And how we rue our haste, finding the gilded morsel to contain a hook. Even so, I think there is some virtue in eagerness, whether its object prove true or false. How utterly dull would be a wholly prudent man, or trout, or world!

My fishing life, and I suspect those of many others, has been a testament to the sort of imprudence Leopold forgave and celebrated. I often arrive at the stream full of haste and eagerness, anxious for the first cast and the first sign of an imprudent trout. If a calmer pace is called for, I have to force upon myself the discipline of watchfulness. Unlike our famous angling masters, who have counseled extended sessions of careful observation, I'm likely to cast first and ask questions later. I'm just too energized for the stingily hoarded casts so eloquently recommended by Vincent Marinaro, and though I heed Walton's admonition to 'study to be quiet', I rarely study to sit still.

Contradictorily, even while I'm so absorbed in finding the next cast, my attention may drift and scatter far beyond the stream's banks. I am taken with the serendipitously eventful quality of life along the stream, with things well removed from the catching of

trout. Leopold's 'new thing' is, for me, the relentless series of surprises and wonders I find in wild nature and moving water. There is too much to do here – too much to absorb, savor, and remember.

It has been said – and not only about fishing – that reading and thinking and talking about something are what we do when we are unable to do the thing itself. The point of this seems to be that such activities are mere consolation until the real thing is available again. That falls short of explaining how fishing works for me. The sport's sages tell us that the thoughtful angler is always studying and learning while fishing, but I seem to organize the whole business differently.

For me, fishing is when I soak up huge amounts of raw experience, renewed wonder, and unprocessed information, and not fishing is when I put my mind to work on that undifferentiated accumulation of impressions. When fishing occupies my nonfishing time, it isn't just a way of killing time until I can actually fish again. It's a way of catching up on all the parts of fishing I can't do when I'm too busy casting. This may not be the best way to go about the thing – certainly it would dismay the sport's role models – but it's involuntary anyway, so I go with it. It's when I study to be quiet.

And sometimes it works really well. It took the preoccupying mechanics of photography and an unfishable section of trout stream to finally make me look hard at how trout feed. And even then, I spent far less time on the stream getting the photographs than I have spent examining those pictures and comparing my impressions with those of the writers and scientists who had previously studied feeding trout – and the fly-fishing theorists who have tried to reason out what it was about a fly or technique that caused the trout to rise in the first place.

And it was only then, as I sorted through all this lore, history, and data, that I began to feel qualified to look back freshly on my own many years of experience with rising trout. The new thing will always be weighed and tested against all the old things.

* * *

Downstream and across, from Bennett Peaks, North Platte River, Wyoming

I am pleased to admit that I am at heart a rather lazy fisherman and have never felt obliged to turn my entire fishing life into an empirical inquiry. In the urgency of arriving at the stream, I am as likely to start with a fly that I am fond of – or excited about because I just tied it – as a fly predicted to work by the prevailing hatch charts. I have fished a lot and for a long time, but nobody is going to take me for one of those hard-driving problem solvers – those admirable and athletic souls whose entire beings are engaged in perfecting fly patterns and presenting them flawlessly.

And yet I always have been enchanted by wild trout and our persistent, quixotic, and sometimes brilliant attempts to understand them well enough to catch them. There is nothing shallow about this enchantment. My approach to fly theory may be somewhat more reflective or even whimsical than those of the hard drivers, but luckily there are many ways to be serious about fishing.

We might casually think of the centuries of fly fishing that preceded us as rather like a long version of our own experiences, in which fly fishers have gradually become smarter and more proficient as the sport has aged. For many generations, the literature of fly fishing has been produced by people who obviously considered themselves substantially wiser than their predecessors. Though 'progress' is as slippery a notion in fishing as it is in many other realms, sometimes those anglers may even have been right about their achievements.

But the comparison between the history of fly fishing and the career of a single fly fisher works another way. Just as most of what any generation of fly fishers knows has been passed down to them by their predecessors, so too do we individuals typically spend much, if not most, of our time learning – rediscovering, if you like – what has been learned countless times before.

Thus we build our sport's long tradition and our own fly-fishing wisdom in a happily complicated series of tiny increments, most of which don't take us in any clearly discernible direction, and some of which have nothing to do with the catching of fish. It's one big, gloriously sloppy experiment. There are indeed those discoveries that we like to think of as progress, but there are also false starts, embarrassments, and dead ends galore. That most of what we learn is not new does not lessen the personal excitement and satisfaction we find in each freshly earned insight. That some of what we learn is probably wrong is just part of the fun. What seems to matter most in this clumsy process is the unpredictable interplay of what we're told with the revelations of what we discover on our own. Aldo Leopold also said, 'The only prudence in fishermen is that designed to set the stage for taking yet another, and perhaps a longer, chance.'

Which is my way of saying that although any fishing book – including and especially this one – may not tell you many truly 'new things', it should at least tell you a few. It should also give you a new look at many old things. And it should invite you to think about all these new and old things in your own way, so you can better make the experiment your own.

Paul Schullery, *On Matthew Bird Creek*, 2006

The Trickle

Until I encountered the Trickle, I had fondly believed that the Pang was about the limit in jungle fishing.

There I had to cast my fly over four rows of flags to reach a run on the far side, had to strike at the sound of the rise and to guide my hooked and very active fish through openings in each of the four rows to my own bank, avoiding en route drifting brambles, cut weed, heavy celery beds, snags, and almost every conceivable hazard of the trout brook.

But the Trickle was a revelation. It carried excess to excess. I think that in the two miles or so of its length which I was privileged to (I was going to say fish) see – no, that is pitching it too high – investigate, it contained less accessible water than any stream of its length and width of channel in the country. For the Trickle has run wild, and in the course of years has lapsed from the status of a clean and tidy little stream irrigating well managed water meadows, into an almost prehistoric stage of neglect, oozing fitfully through overgrown spongy banks of sphagnum, peering through openings in dense beds of celery and watercress, and only showing its real width at rare intervals where, for instance, horses, turned out to crop the rough pasture afforded by its meadows, have beaten down the banks and water growths and made a clearing in crossing to and fro.

Yet, for all its handicaps, the Trickle holds trout, astonishingly good trout for its size – and wary and wild as hawks.

It was at one of these horse fords that I first encountered the little stream, having determined to cross it and make a circuit to reach the wire fence which formed the bottom boundary of my leave, and fish it from the right bank to avoid exposing myself on the higher ground which sloped down to the left margin. So I stepped into the water, and straightway sent scuttling to cover a trout of a good pound and a smaller satellite. The water nowhere reached above my ankles as I crossed, and four or five steps took me to the other side. Above and below the ford the stream quickly contracted to a couple of feet, so far, at any rate, as exposed surface went.

In my circuit of a hundred yards or so to reach the jumping off place I put up a snipe, a hare, and a brace of rabbits; indeed the meadows of its course abound with snipe, and the rough shooting must be very good. At the bottom, where the stream finds its way through a culvert under a railway line it is almost open for ten or twelve twisted yards, above which it receives a tributary dribble,

and here it runs perhaps a yard wide and a foot or more deep. An injudicious exposure of my head sent a three-quarter-pounder to cover and disturbed a second fish which shot up the dribble, but as my Sedge fly lit on the surface of the little pool just above the junction it met with an immediate response from a game little eleven-inch trout which gave me some trouble before I lifted him out. The season of 1916 was a bad one, and I was not out for a basket, so I unhooked him gently and released him.

Above the little pool just mentioned, the stream disappeared for some yards. One had to force one's way through a tangle of man-high flowering reed, taking care by probing with the landing handle not to step up to the knee into the hidden channel of the little stream. Presently at a bend a run of five or six feet long with a width of nine inches to a foot between cress bed and water musk became visible. Luckily there was no wind, and the little nine-footer was built for short and accurate casting. So it was possible to fish up the little run foot by foot. Sure enough at the bend up came a 12½ in fish and fastened. Heroic measures were necessary and were applied, and soon his head was up and he was slid over the cress bed into the net, to be unhooked and turned down stream.

Just round the bend the water opened a little, and standing uneasily on a bed of quaking mud, punctuated thickly with flags, I dropped the fly in front of a good 1¼ lb trout which lay out on a bit of bare gravel. He looked at it suspiciously, and at the end of the second offer he had it, but not soundly, for as he dashed down stream under my feet the fly came away, and I lost the best trout I saw that day.

Above, the marginal growth closed over the little stream once more and for quite a stretch it was invisible and consequently unfishable. Then I came to the place below the ford, and I looked carefully to see if my pound friend had come out from his shelter. He had, but he was obviously disturbed in his mind. However, I had no time to waste while he calmed down. So I offered him the sedge. Unfortunately, I had forgotten his companion, a little yellow half-pounder, and on my line falling over him, he bolted up stream and sent the larger fish scurrying up the ford and into a weed bed above.

Between the ford and the next fence, a matter of half-a-hundred yards, I found four or five little foot-wide runs and extracted and returned trout of 9 and 10 inches from two of them. At the fence the water came through a little hatch, and there another trout flashed at my fly, and escaped the barb. Above for a full quarter of a mile the water was stiff with flags of enormous size so that nowhere was there any channel where one could cast a fly nor any current, and after a gap of half-a-dozen yards, where a little surface might be seen, there was another stretch of flag-ridden jungle. But in the gap there was a waiting trout of a pound or more. Unfortunately he caught sight of me before I caught sight of him.

Warned by this error I was more cautious in approaching the next gap and was rewarded by the capture of a beautiful yellow 11 in trout. Then after another stretch of jungle I came upon another phase of the Trickle. Here the base of hard gravel on which it cut through spongy soil was nearer to the surface than it was lower down, and the flags ceased to flourish. But the water-cress beds throve amazingly on either side, constricting the channel of brightly running water to the width of a foot. Here a few casts showed me that the trout ran much smaller, and I pushed on to the next meadows, taking a cast here and there in the more likely corners and in a couple of hatch-holes and below a culvert.

But the next meadow…

And the next…

Jungle, jungle, jungle to the sky line.

So I reeled up.

But after all I had not had so bad a morning on the Trickle, and I look back with pleasure to my visit to that little stream.

And I hope that when the war is over and the lessees set themselves in earnest to improve their little fishery they will not let zeal outrun discretion, but will preserve where they can, consistently with providing a channel for fishing the naive and unaffected wildness which makes the little water so charming.

G.E.M. Skues, *The Chalkstream Angler*, 1932

Trout by Richard Smith

Trout... and a Salmon

There was once a young man in a shooting lodge among the misty red hills and it was Lammas time. And the rain roared and hammered on roof and windows and, on such a day as yon, you would not be driving a grouse were it ever so. And the young man could not play at bridge for he had not the bridge faculty. But neither had he a fishing rod, for he had come to shoot grouse and not to catch burn trouts.

So he stood in the window and listened to the singing of the showers. And he went to the hall door and opened it, and the West Wind, sweet with the rain and the smell of the pinewoods, went by with a shout and bade him follow it. It was then that his host told that, if a body walked two miles over the hill, that he would come to the Logie Water wherein were trout for the catching. The rod to take them on was still the difficulty. But a rod was borrowed from the bothy. It was a little old two-piece trout rod and it was lashed with binding and bound about with twine. But it was light and whippy and the handicraft of a great maker of old, and Peter Stuart had had it in a present from 'her Leddyship' at Druim this long time ago.

But the young man was not concerned for the genesis of the rod so long as he might get a loan of it. And to this he was kindly welcome. There was a 'sufficiency' of line on the reel too. And, as it passed the not too drastic testing of a line, all was well. Peter had some bait hooks and a yard or two of gut. The procuring of a 'pucklie' worms, in wet moss and a mustard tin, would not hinder long. And so the guest was provided for. And presently he swung a game bag upon his back, for creel there was none, and, syne, he was for away. But not before he had remembered that, in the cap to match with his Lovat mixture of yesterday's wearing, there were two or three trout flies. So it was that cap that he would put on. And before he did so he asked about the Logie Water, for he knew it not.

The Logie was, it appeared, a wee stony water on most days and the trout that lived in it were wee trout. About six to the pound? They would be just about that, said the angler's host. But they were plump and golden little trout and dusted on with crimson spots, and sometimes, maybe, there was a half pounder to be had. The Logie ran into the Waupie of course. And the Waupie was a salmon river? Why, yes, the Waupie was a salmon river, but no salmon were ever in the Logie because they could not get up the Linn of Logie. And a very good reason too, thought the angler as he crossed the hill. And the West Wind was blowing steady and the rain was going out on it. But the hills were full of the roar of waters where the burns ran foaming full. And the mist rose out of the glens and the curries and shifted, like grey smoke, and through it the hills, what a man might see of them, were very dark and blue. And when the angler got to the Logie Water he thought that it was a real bonny little river.

Like all the hill waters the Logie rose like a rocket. But she cleared soon and then she ran in good and swirling ply for a whole fishing day before she fell in and went trickling among the humpbacked stones that huddled in the course of her like a herd of sheep that lie in a park. But there were none of these river sheep to show today. A sleek back here and a sleek back there perhaps, a swirl, a curl, a brown eddy to mark, you'd say, a likely cast, a likely resting place for a running fish. That is, did salmon run the Logie. But no salmon ever ran the Logie because none, as we know, may mount the Linn of Logie. Which was a sad pity, said the angler, for it is a pretty little river, this Logie, and if he, the angler, were Lord Pittenweem, his host's landlord, he'd have the Linn, and the rocks that made it roar, dynamited out of that and a passage made for my lord the salmon.

'This is no worm water, anyhow', thought the fisherman. And he sat down and considered the flies that he wore in his bonnet. There, tied on gut, were a male March brown, a red palmer, two teals-and-red, and a couple more that he could put no name to. 'They'll serve,' said he, 'and if I fish them single they'll see me through the day.' So our angler took the worms out of the mustard tin and howked a hole and buried them, moss and all; for he was a young man solicitous of all living things. He mounted the March brown, the March brown that kills well everywhere and, in spite of its specialist title, all the year round.

As he makes his first cast, a slant of sun kisses the water simultaneously with his March brown, and an ouzel speeds upstream and under the angler's very line. The angler notes the pucker where the March brown alights on the Logie Water, and almost before that miniature ring has disappeared there is a flash of gold at the fly. The angler twitches the rod top, but the trout has missed the March brown. To the repeated cast the fingerling responds with a dash and, hooking himself, tears, for all that he weighs scarce the poor quarter of a pound, a goodly yard of line

off a stiffish reel. He is beached (for the angler has never a net) where the Logie, fringed with a lace of foam, sweeps round a tiny curve of sand and small gravel.

The report on the trouts of the Logie has been a true report. This is a remarkable pretty trout, fat and well-liking, high in the shoulder, deep in the golden flank and dotted upon, as it was said that he would be, in crimson dots. So, with a quick tap on his head, the coup de grâce that every takeable trout should get ere he be basketed, the game bag receives him to lie upon two handfuls of hill grass and heather. He is not long alone there for, to the next cast, there is a glancing rise and a trout that might be the twin of the first is making her Leddyship's little rod bend and curtsey as he leaps and leaps again. A game and a gallant little fighter he is, but in a minute or so he also is drawn up on to the little circle of sand and his troubles, if ever he had any until now, are over.

The sun is hot by this time and the wet heather is steaming in the kindliness of light and day. The angler can hear the pop of guns somewhere over the march. The tenant of Waupie Lodge has evidently gone to the hill for an after luncheon hour or two. But our friend is very well content to be where he is. The little Logie trout are worth a lot of grouse and, moreover, none so little as all that are some of them. For on the edge of a smooth break, a streaming swirl that marks the sunken boulder, Troll-tossed a million years ago from a mountain top to lie for all time in Logie as the shelter of great trout, the March brown is taken with a devil of a tug. And almost before the angler can raise the point of her Leddyship, for, as such, he has come to know lovingly the little engine at his command, a great trout, every ounce of three-quarters of a pound, fat as butter, golden as guineas, leaps with a shattering leap and, falling with a splash, has gone and the March brown with him.

Well now, that's a pity and all, but there are over two dozen trout in the game bag and an uncommon pretty creel they are and uncommon well, no doubt, they will taste, split and fried and eaten with cold fresh butter and a sprig of parsley. And talking of eating it is now three-thirty and the angler has not yet eaten the egg sandwiches that Maggie came running after him with as he went out. He will eat them now therefore. And that done, shall it be the Palmer as a second horse, or one of the anonymous insects – or a teal-and-red?

A teal-and-red it is, and now the angler will catch another five trout to make the three dozen and then be facing the lodge-ward two miles up along the March burn, over the rigging, down hill again, and so home. This pool is a real picture of a pool and it is a thousand sorrows that salmon cannot loup the Linn of Logie, for, if they could, you'd say, in this water, that it is here you'd get into a fish. The river shoots and tumbles in peacock tails of amber, over an upheaval of granite it goes, with a flounce of foam, and so, into a deep, fast, porter-coloured pool – a pool that thins out on to a wide shallow of gravel that, in turn, contracts into the rough-and-tumble neck of another important-looking piece of water.

Very quickly the angler catches a further three of the game little trout to whom he has grown accustomed. And the teal-and-red now explores the glassy honey-coloured glide, the fan of clearing water, and it all happens in a second of time, there is a welt of sudden silver that shoots athwart just where the teal-and-red – ah, no salmon can loup – but 'her Leddyship's' slight nose is pulled, for all that, most savagely a-down and the line goes off the stiff reel with a shriek.

Twenty yards out and the hooked fish, finding the shallow, throws himself sideways out of the water, clean and beautiful and swift, the salmon who has louped the Linn – the sea-silver salmon who has established a precedent! And back he comes into the dark water with a clash that takes him upstream, up till almost he'd leave the pool at the top of it. Indeed, for a moment he hangs in the very tumult of the entry, then as the angler comes opposite to him, he goes down, down under the boughs of the birks on the far bank and the line buzzing like bees.

Splash, he is on the shallow once more. He jolts and he lunges, and then 'her Leddyship' is pulled almost straight as the rough water at the neck of the next pool takes charge of the fish. Headlong down he goes and headlong the angler follows after him – fifty dividing yards after him, fifty of the sixty yards of line that the reel runs to. The next pool is a bonny pool too – bonny from an artistic point of view anyhow – but rock-staked and swirling, a bad place to beat a fish in. And beaten he must be, for at the tail of this pool boils the Linn itself and plunges over and down in spouts of waterfalls. However, there is seventy yards of water to go or ever the fish may make the fall, and half-way thereto is a bit of shelving gravel and backwater which the angler notes well. The fish, 6 lb is he, 8 perhaps, has had a rattling and if he can be brought to the gravel the rod shall do yet. And so her 'Leddyship' bends and condescends with all her slim might.

And gradually the fish comes to her, heavily now and sometimes with the wedge of his steel-grey tail cutting the surface. The angler holds him as tightly as he dares, gives him such of the butt as he presumes. And the gods are on his side, for, rolling this way and that way, the fish comes to hand. And the angler, with a last guiding pressure, lays him, head and shoulders, on the beach, and dropping 'her Leddyship', he tails the only salmon that ever louped Logie's Linn.

Patrick Chalmers, *The Linn of Logie*, 1931

Nearing the net by Henry Alken

Dace on the Fly

The angler might travel very much farther and fare very much worse. That is my thought every time I visit Isleworth fly-rod in hand, and it is strange if September or October does not find me there at least once in each year. I have made the expedition pretty often now, but the charm of it never fails; it is like nothing that I know in the way of fishing near London. Nowhere else can one feel that one is literally cheating Fate out of a few happy hours.

When one goes farther afield, to the Colne, perhaps, at West Drayton, Uxbridge, or Rickmansworth, there is the sense of an undertaking about it; one is earning the right to enjoyment by dint of railway travelling, by having made 'arrangements', by being burdened with a landing net and possibly lobworms – one is definitely out for the day. But Isleworth is a simple, unpremeditated sort of matter. At luncheon time one has a sudden conviction that too much work is telling on one's health, and that an afternoon off is the right medicine. A glance at the paper tells one that the tide was high at London Bridge at half-past nine; a simple calculation proves that, since it is an hour later at Richmond, the Isleworth shallows will begin to be fishable at about two.

A light ten-foot rod, a reel, fly box, and basket take no long time to collect; the rubber knee-boots stand ready in their corner. One is equipped and away almost as soon as the idea has been formed.

It matters little that the train stops at all stations, and that the carriages are primitive almost to archaism. En route for Richmond these things are just and proper. One likes to see people getting in and out full of business. Even if one does not quite understand why anyone living in Gunnersbury should apparently be in such a hurry, so impatient to get to Kew Gardens and urgent affairs, this does not mar the sense of personal emancipation; rather it enhances it by contrast.

One could get out at Kew Gardens oneself, by the way, walk down to the towpath, and fish up to Isleworth, and I have done this once or twice. But I prefer on the whole to go on to Richmond now and walk downstream. Richmond has made efforts of late to get into line with the times, but mercifully its fascination will not easily be destroyed. Modernity mellows there by the side of age better than in almost any place I know. As a matter of fact, one sees little of the town, for almost opposite the station yard is a gate leading to the old deer park. It is about ten minutes' walk across the park to the towpath, which one strikes just above the lock, and yet ten minutes more to the church ferry at the bottom of Isleworth Eyot. Above the lock there are always anglers, but I have never yet seen one of them actually catch anything at the time of my passing. From below it one can see the weir, the only one on the Thames which has not moved in me the desire of trout. At high water, however, it looks as if it ought to hold one or two, and there certainly are trout in the reach, though systematic trout-fishing does not seem to go on there. I remember once seeing a big trout feed at the head of the Eyot, but whether he is still in existence I know not. Almost any day at low water, however, below the Eyot there are alarms and excursions to be seen among the dace, which argue fish of prey of considerable size, trout probably. Occasionally, too, a trout is caught by a dace-fisher, but it is usually a small one.

Arrived at the ferry, it is well to cross over and fish on the other side, and the knowledgeable make their way down for a third of a mile or perhaps rather more to the point where the river is shallowest, just above a slight but recognisable bend in the stream. Here, they say, are the biggest dace, the 6 oz fish, which, when caught, are to be found at the top in each man's basket, like ½ lb trout in Devonshire. But I should say that there is a fair sprinkling of these big dace all the way down, the difficulty being to catch them. Some men hold by big flies, coachmen, black gnats, yellow duns, etc., on No. 1 or even No. 2 hooks being considered about right, and more than once I have been tempted to the same opinion. Lately, however, the big fly has not served me well. On my last visit nothing but a black spider on a tiny hook would do any good. That afternoon also upset another theory, or, rather, taught me something new. My belief had been that you could catch the Isleworth dace in two ways – one with the dry or semi-dry fly, in which case the fish usually took it on the drop or half volley, as some authority puts it, or wet and drawn along more or less rapidly under water. For a while they confirmed me in this belief, and I caught several with the dry fly, while I missed a good many in the other way.

On the way to fish by Walter Dendy Sadler

Then they ceased to come up to it at all, either wet or dry, until I accidentally got a rise in recovering the fly as it floated. This led to experiments, and I found that, by letting the fly fall dry and then dragging it for a few inches along the surface, I got plenty of rises, and pretty bold ones too. The fish came at it before it had gone 6 in or not at all, and for an hour I had quite a brisk bit of sport, so much so that on reaching the ferry I did not hesitate to estimate the number of fish kept as three dozen. I was really surprised, on counting tails afterwards, to find that there were only a dozen and a half. It had seemed to me that for a time I was catching them as fast as I could. Three dozen would be a very fair basket for a good day, though takes of eight or ten dozen are made once in a way. Six inches is the size limit, and the majority of fish caught are about seven. If your three dozen average 3 oz apiece, you have done very well indeed, and if you have three or four 6 oz fish you may be proud. There are plenty of these big ones in the water, but they are difficult to tempt.

It is worth while catching a dish of these little dace, if only for the pleasure of looking at them afterwards. They make a brave silvery show when laid side by side, and though individually at time of capture they have not the looks of brook trout, collectively in the evening they have the advantage. Brook trout lose their gold, but dace preserve their silver. One good angler informed me (rather apologetically), that he proposed to have his catch to breakfast. No apology was needed, for, bones admitted and extracted, dace are good meat – as good as many trout.

But dace are not the whole of Isleworth fishing. There is the daily wonder of the great river shrinking away so that a man may go dry-foot (or practically so) along its gravel bed, to see only a clear, shallow stream where a few hours back was a deep, turbid flood; there is the awful pleasure of imagining what would happen if one were caught suddenly by the turn of the tide, for one is so low down in the world that it seems well-nigh impossible to climb up that steep bank through the mud to the grounds of Syon House; there is the wonderful solitude almost within sound of London – a small human figure or so up at the ferry, perhaps, and about the brown-sailed barges at the distant quay, but for the rest no sign of life except a gull or two wheeling round, some rooks exploring the naked river bed, and the dace dimpling the surface of the quiet stream.

Then, when the tide has turned (and may you be not too far from the ferry when that happens!), there is a late tea at the London Apprentice, the quaint old inn near the church. The view from its billiard room window up stream and down is alone worth the journey. After it there is the return in the ferry boat, with a long backward look at the riverside street and the old church beneath their canopy of crimson sky; the meditative walk back along the towpath under the great trees, almost each one sheltering its couple of shy lovers who are making believe that the world is as they would have it be; the crossing of the old green, with its circle of fair dwellings; and lastly, the extraordinary blaze of light as one gets to the corner of the green and looks up towards the town. This is a fitting end to a day of impressions that one does not easily forget.

H.T. Sheringham, *An Open Creel,* 1910

Trout

Chalkstream Fighters

The number of trout in different parts of the Itchen and Test is in inverse proportion to their weight; but in the parts of these rivers where the trout are not overcrowded and average from 1½ to 2 lb, they rise freely and their appearance in a good season is splendid.

The extraordinary fatness to which they attain, and the brilliancy of their colour and condition in May, June and July, surpass anything it has been my good fortune to see amongst river trout, and anything I could have believed, if I had fished only in north country rivers. On the other hand, the chalk stream trout do not fight so strongly in proportion to their size as the trout in rocky or swifter rivers with rougher water and no weeds. It is not that the southern trout is less strong, but it thinks too much of the weeds: it is always trying to hide itself instead of trying to get free by wild desperate rushes, for which indeed the presence of the weeds and the gentleness of the water make these rivers less suited. Sometimes the first rush of a chalk stream trout when hooked is as sudden and wild and strong as that of a fish of the same size in any other river; but in my experience this generally happens with a south country trout when its feeding place is far down on a shallow or in a long mill-tail, and its home is in the hatch-hole or under the mill above. In such places I have known a trout of 1½ lb leave very few yards of line upon the reel before its first rush could be checked, and the line to be run out as swiftly and as straight as any one could wish. Twice during the last season did it happen to me to have fine experiences of this kind. In the first case the trout had

something over twenty yards to go for safety, and nearly succeeded. Had the distance been two or three yards less it would have been accomplished in the first rush, but in the last few yards the trout had to collect his strength for a second effort. There was a moment's break in the impetus of the rush, and a struggle began in which at first the trout gained ground, but very slowly, while every foot was contested with the utmost pressure that I dared put upon the gut: then there ceased to be progress, and at last within close sight of his home the trout had to turn his head. The rest was easy, the mill-tail being fairly clear of weeds, and both time and stream being against the fish.

In the second case the result was different. I was wading in a shallow where I could see the trout, which, as it turned out, was never to be mine. It was a light-coloured fish feeding actively and recklessly on the flies, which were coming down freely, and it took my fly at once with perfect confidence. It sometimes happens, however, that these active, reckless, easily hooked trout are more surprised and desperate when hooked than any others. I never saw anything more mad and sudden than the rush of this trout. It gained a pool below some hatches, where no doubt it lived, and took the line under the rough main stream into a fine whirling

Small stream fishing, engraving

back-water: then I felt the confusion of having lost touch with the fish, for there was nothing but the dull sodden strain of a line hopelessly drowned in the contending currents of the hatch-hole. The trout jumped high in the middle of the pool, and showed me that, if under 2 lb, he was certainly very thick and strong; I dropped the point of the rod without being able to give the least relief to the fine gut at the end, and the stream swept downwards a useless length of submerged line without a fly.

Sir Edward Grey, *Fly Fishing,* 1907

The Benign Moment

The benign moment is difficult to define or explain, though every fisherman knows it. It is like one of those sudden silences in a general conversation when, in England, we say, 'An angel passes' and in Russia, in the old days, they used to say, 'A policeman is being born'. The day is not that day but another. Everything feels and looks different.

The fisherman casts not in the mere hope of rising a fish but, knowing that he will rise one, concerned only to hook it when it comes. He knows that even the hooking of it is more likely than at other times. Weather, river and fish seem suddenly to be on the angler's side and prepared to do their best for him. This is not the moment to be wasted in putting on a fresh cast. Hawthorn trees seem to know this and, joining in the happy conspiracy, skilfully evade the flies that in moments not benign they reach out to clutch greedily behind the angler's back. Or is it that in these moments, trout rise so near the fisherman that he is never tempted to lengthen his line in dangerous places? But in other moments all places are dangerous. Flies cling to moss, to stones, to clothing, whirl themselves tightly round the rod or, in an instant, turn a straight piece of fine gut into a cat's cradle.

When this last happens, wise fishermen take it as a kindly indication that the moment is not benign and that their flies may as well not be on the water. If they swear they do so with such good temper and even gratitude that their words fall like a caress.

They do not pull off the cast to be disentangled at home, but, there and then, sit down patiently at the riverside, observe with calm pleasure a wagtail or a dipper, enlarge their souls to leisure, and, without hurry, reduce the cat's cradle to order, stretch the cast anew and know that they have lost no time, no good time, at all. And when this elaborate business is finished, if they do not arise suddenly with violence and stride with determination up-stream, they have a good chance of being rewarded in other coin beside that of moral satisfaction in which, already, they have been richly paid. Half a dozen sand-martins may be skimming the water, picking up from above their share of a hatch of flies that the trout will be attacking from below.

More: trout may be rising in the very water which the angler left when he came ashore to do his disentangling. The fish that was put down by being offered the tangle of gut that it was not his business to unravel, may now be rising again and ready to take

Studying the river, by Ernest Briggs

the fly that was in that tangle, now happily straightened out. Again and again it happens that the benign moment follows immediately upon a moment so far from benign that it has compelled the fisherman to give the river a rest.

So often, indeed, does this happen that I am sometimes tempted to think that the benign moment is a wholly subjective affair, that it is less a state of river than a state of mind and that when we are told to take a rest when we are fishing badly, we are really being told to create, artificially, a benign moment for ourselves. But, when actually fishing, I am quite sure that the benignity of the happy moment, when it comes, is not of my making, is not dependent upon me and is dependent on some subtle combination of circumstances not under my control. It is a meteorological, not a psychological phenomenon. And with that I am back again at the difficulty, not so much of defining it as of explaining it, of analysing it into its component parts. I sometimes fancy that it depends on some slight change in atmospheric pressure. This would explain why it seems not only to make the trout more willing to rise and to take flies well into the back of their mouths, but also to improve the fisherman.

I fancy that if, in addition to all the tackle we already carry with us (we could not do it if we had as many fish to carry as our grandfathers), we had with us barographs of sensitive nature, registering changes of pressure so that we could observe them from hour to hour and even from minute to minute, we should find that the benign moments of which we were conscious would be marked in some way in the line traced by the barograph's recording needle. Those moments are not to be explained simply as coincident with a hatch of fly. In moments other than benign flies may sail down river in Armadas without the slightest effect on our baskets. And, in any case, how judge between cause and effect? A hatch of fly does usually seem to accompany a benign moment, but may not the flies, like the trout and the fisherman, be encouraged by the moment instead of being its cause?

Then, too, on our swiftly varying rivers, it is possible that prolonged observation would show that the benign moments would be indicated in some way on a curve that should represent from minute to minute the rising and falling of the water. For example, a benign moment often occurs when the river first shows to the fish signs that it is going to rise. To the fish, I say, for they know all about it before the duller angler has drawn his deductions from the flotsam carried on the stream, the first dry leaves picked from its shores as the river, higher up, brimmed above the line at which they had been left. And when, after a freshet, the river clears, such moments are sometimes to be enjoyed. But here, we seem to be considering good conditions for angling in general rather than the conditions of those rare moments that sometimes make the difference between a blank day and one on which the returning angler sings or whistles in the dusk. The benign moment proper occurs, and is most noticeable when it does occur, in a day on which the conditions for fishing are, in general, poor.

Perhaps on account of our unsettled weather and uncertain streams, the benign moment may be considered as a phenomenon characteristic of north country fishing. On the equable chalk streams it occurs, but is, somehow, less important. On the prettiest chalk stream in England I have known a dull hour to be followed by this miraculous change, as if I had closed my eyes for a moment and opened them on a different day, as if a wand had been waved and a spell loosed by some invisible being in the water-meadows. In the south, however, the coming or not coming of the benign moment is not one of the chief interests in the day. Whereas, with us, the possibility of its coming is the thing that enables us to put up with much hardship and disappointment. In this weather, with the barometer jumping up and down like a grasshopper, with the river one foot in drought and one in flood, to one thing constant never, the hope of the benign moment sustains the fisherman through many barren hours and sometimes puts something in his basket at the end of them.

Arthur Ransome, *Rod and Line*, 1929

Watercraft

The type of small stream you start out on, and fish most often, will shape your primary set of small-stream skills. The water itself will hone your abilities; you don't have to pay conscious attention to the matter, though it might help.

If the stream is of the mountain sort, you'll become better adept at creeping close, staying out of sight, casting short, dancing trout in abruptly. If you begin on a foothill stream, you'll get better and better at taking an unobtrusive position at the foot of a pool, assessing it for the most likely holding lies, making accurate casts, and getting drag-free drifts. If your early water is of the meadow stream sort, you'll get good at hanging back, making accurate observations, then presenting your fly delicately when you've spotted some activity.

None of these skills is entirely separate and applicable on just one type of water. What serves you well on one type of small stream will work at times, and in certain sections, on all the others. To become a well-rounded small-water angler, adept on all water types, you need to develop the full set of skills that works best for each of them and is then transportable to all of them.

The best way to acquire those skills is to fish small waters as often as you can, in as many different places as possible, and let small waters of all types shape your various skills for you. Then in any situation you get into, you'll know precisely which ability to apply.

Salmon, by Neil Dalrymple

Dave Hughes, *Trout and Stream, 2002*

Autumn Stillwater

There are two kinds of trout at Blagdon: day fish and night fish; and three kinds of anglers – day anglers, night anglers, and day and night anglers, or anglers of iron. The night angler begins fishing at about 8 p.m. The time of his finishing is not revealed. One can understand his being. There is a particular fascination about fishing at night which appeals to minds that love to dream and delight in mystery; there is a bogeyness in black water, there is something aweing in the moon-streaked lake, which draws some men just as danger attracts the brave; hence the night angler at Blagdon. He uses large flies, and casts a short, thick line along the edge, and takes the fish stationed there on the look-out for sticklebacks. He is often very successful.

The day angler is of a different type. He is a sunny fellow, delighting in the wide sweep of heaven, the rolling cloud, the shadows chasing each other across the ruffled water, the dappled hills, the green fields, the birds, flowers, and great insect world; he likes to see the great fish plunge after his fly: he likes a fair fight on fine tackle. He is often not successful.

The day and night angler is, in truth, a variety of the day angler. He is an unsuccessful day angler of great strength of both mind and body who greatly desires a fish, and who continues fishing far into the night with this object in view. He is greatly to be admired. He often deservedly secures his desire. There is still another kind of angler – a fisher of dry and small flies. He is a poor fool, who is under the delusion that Blagdon fish can thus be caught, given favourable conditions; but, of course, the favourable conditions never come – thus his foolishness. Four years ago these conditions occurred on a Sunday – or was it a dream? The Blagdon trout rose to a fish; the estimated catch was eight fish, weighing 32 lb. Each year the pitiable angler returns, hoping against hope, as the lover to meet his beloved, where the great waves from out of the west beat barrenly on the rock-bound shore.

Trout over gravel, acrylic by Richard Smith

Year one he had some slight success; he slew, on a dry fly, the largest fish in two seasons. Year two was not barren of sport. Year three was last year, and this is what he did:

The weather conditions for dry-fly fishing were, on the whole, good. There were calm, warm days, when the lake was either wholly or partially glass-like. The evenings were calm and warm, but rising fish were very rare. This was entirely due to a great dearth of fly on the water. This absence of fly may possibly be due

to the presence of great numbers of sticklebacks. In past seasons only odd sticklebacks were seen, but that year they cruised about the shallows in shoals, no doubt seeking out and devouring the insect life under water. The olive midge and green midge, which in the past caused good rises of fish, were almost rare; the small grey sedge fly not common. One fly, however, was more common

– the olive dun. On several days between 11.30 a.m. and 1 p.m. there were good hatches of this fly, and a few fish were found taking them.

At Blagdon there are both brown and rainbow trout. The brown can be at once dismissed, because during a whole week not one was even seen to rise.

The rainbow trout are not distributed, like the brown, all over the lake, but are concentrated at a few places where there is deep water; four such places were found – the top of the second boat-house bay, the Butcombe end of the dam, the top of Butcombe Bay, and Butcombe Point. At these, during the morning, whilst olive duns were hatching out, and at evening, when a few green and olive midges were on the water, a few rainbows were found rising. These fish were attacked in one of two ways, depending on how often the fish were rising. If they were rising frequently, from a distance and before approaching to the water, the course of their cruising was first noted; fish rising in still water always cruise, and always follow a definite course, up and down or round and round in circles, triangles, oblongs, etc.; choice is then made of a suitable spot for the dry fly, so that when the fish comes round he will come to it, and, it is hoped, take it. The line, cast, and fly must be well oiled, so as to float permanently on the water.

The first fish caught, a 3 lb 2 oz rainbow, gave an excellent example of this method of attack. This fish was taking olive midges in a small circle at the top of the second boathouse bay; an olive midge was placed on the rim of this circle; the first time round the fish passed under it; the second a great nose appeared by the fly, then a back and a tail – the fly was gone. The line tightened, and a heavy fish was felt. The battle was rather drawn out, because the gut was 3X, and was full of anxiety because of the weeds. However, a good fish was at last landed.

If the fish be rising at infrequent intervals, other tactics must be employed, for it is impossible to map out the course of a rising fish if it be rising perhaps only once every ten minutes. This is the procedure: take up a position near the rising fish, wait till the fish rises, note during the rise the direction in which the fish is heading, hurriedly place the fly in front of it. In the vast majority of cases nothing will happen; presently the fish will be seen to rise again, at once the fly is picked off the water and replaced as before; if again no response is made, the angler must wait for the next rise of the fish, and then cast as before, and so on until the fly is taken. It is unwise to make a cast when the position of the fish is not known, because of the danger of unwittingly dropping the fly or cast close to it and putting it down. If the angler has reason to believe that the fish is passing by his floating fly and not noticing it, he may render it more attractive by twitching his line just enough to make the fly shake, but no more; this will sometimes attract the fish's attention and cause it to deviate from its course towards the angler's fly. By this method, and provided the angler has a good imitation of the natural fly, the fish will probably be captured. But much time is often required; two hours may be spent on such a fish without result. One evening such a fish was found rising at the top of Butcombe Bay, taking green midges which were ovipositing. After one and a half hour's fishing, during which perhaps only ten casts were made, the fish rose at the artificial fly; such a long-deferred rise is liable to make the angler strike too hard, or too soon. This fish was tightened on, not too hard but somewhat too quickly, the result being a lightly hooked fish of about 20 lb, which jumped and jumped and jumped and spluttered along the surface of the water, playing in the most lively fashion. Realising the state of affairs, the angler handled the fish most delicately, at last tired it out, and drew it quietly and slowly shorewards, when almost at the mouth of the net the fish opened wide its jaws, the hook came softly out, and the victim was free. Thus was lost, not any sport, for the fish was dead-beat, but only a good dish.

J.C. Mottram, *Fly-Fishing: Some New Arts and Mysteries,* 1921

On Loch-na-Larich

Hardly a ripple ruffles the surface of beautiful Loch Sween, and the sun shines brilliantly from a blue unclouded sky. What breeze there is comes fitfully from the north-east, and a light haze blots out the familiar view of the Pap of Jura. The gulls float lazily round; one or two terns drop screaming down upon the small fry, and everything looks delightful except to the eye of a fisherman.

But it is not a day for one to stop at home who has only just arrived from London on a short holiday, and the only question for decision is to which of the hill lochs I shall turn my steps. Loch Choilliber holds the largest trout, but it is proverbial that the best chance of sport in its deep waters is 'a regular downright beast of a day', and it is so sheltered by wood and brae that it requires half a gale to produce a good curl upon its bays and inlets. So the pounders may have a rest today, and I determine to content myself with the nearer and more exposed waters of Loch-na-Larich. If I get no sport there a short half-hour's stroll will bring me home again; but although I advance that fact as one of the reasons for my choice, my host laughingly shakes his head, for he knows that it is not at all likely that I shall be back much before dinner-time. However, he wishes me good luck, and I am soon strolling through the wood and up the brae, accompanied by my black spaniel Ben, and by a lad carrying my luncheon, rod, and impedimenta. My mackintosh for once I determine to leave at home.

Travellers who have been in the Holy Land describe the Sea of Galilee as being of the shape of a harp, and the same simile will give a good idea of the little mountain tarn which breaks upon my view in a cup of the hills below Cruach Lussa. There is no bloom yet upon the heather which clothes the moors around it, as it is early June, but the young bracken is shooting up through last year's withered fronds; and the small birch trees which fringe the opposite side of the little bay at the near end are brilliant with their early green. Great kingcups shine like stars among the stones at the side, and the sandpipers busily flit from rock to rock, while the air is musical with their voices, and the louder bubbling breeding-season note of the curlew which hovers over the opposite brae. Two or three mallards fly away as we approach, and a matronly duck leads a numerous brood of some eleven tiny balls of down into the reeds at the far end for shelter. The boat is moored to a small pier below me, padlocked to a chain and rope, and I sit down and put my rod together, while my attendant unfastens the padlock and prepares to get all ready for a start.

And now occurs the first misfortune of the day. The gillie has duly unfastened the padlock, but the chain is broken, and at the first pull it comes away in his hands, leaving the boat still floating out of reach. I ask him what is to be done, and he replies that he must wade for it; and after I have vainly endeavoured to move it by throwing my light line across it, we determine that wading is the only plan likely to succeed. He is for going in at once, accoutred as he is, but I impress upon him that there is no hurry, and he so far indulges my weakness as to consent to take off his shoes and stockings. This does not, however, prevent his getting wet, for the water is not merely well over his knickerbockers, but nearly up to his shoulders, before he is able to reach the boat with a long stick. While he is baling, I see a rise a little to the left, just within reach of the shore, and as I drop my fly with a longish line into the circle, a little fellow rises boldly and takes the dropper, although there is no ripple on the water. I haul him out, pulling and struggling manfully considering his size, and, as I land him, find that there is a second one attached to the tail fly, and that I have caught two with my first cast. They are not so long as my hand, but I do not put them back again, for there are really too many fish in the loch, and it would be a good thing to reduce the stock. Besides, they are excellent for breakfast, and, if I am too particular about size, it is quite probable that there may not be enough for a fry. The ordinary run of fish in this loch is about three to the pound, and one is lucky if one gets one of over a pound in a good day's fishing.

And now commences the familiar but unsatisfactory process of hunting the breeze. We gaze round the loch, and make up our minds that the best chance will be in the little bay under the birches, where there appears to be a tiny ripple. As soon as we arrive there, it has entirely disappeared, and seems to have turned its attention to the very spot we have just left. It is not hard work either for rower or fisherman, and the former just holds the boat within reach of shore, while I keep dropping my three flies as lightly as possible a few yards from the rocks, and am occasionally rewarded with a shy rise, and get a few fish, some of them of quite a decent size. What determined fighters they are! They bend my light rod, and even run out a little line. If the lazy South-Country giants of the Test or Mimram had half their energy and strength,

few indeed in those weedy streams would succumb to the tiny hooks and gossamer gut necessary for effecting their capture at any time but the mayfly season. I see a few alders on the water, and am most successful with an imitation of that fly, dressed pretty large and sunk rather deep. In spite of the weather, I nearly always get an offer from any fish I see rise within reach and manage to put my fly over; but although I strike very quickly, I do not succeed in touching one in three, as they see too much, and turn before they actually touch the fly. One little fish of about ¼ lb is hooked foul, near the ventral fin, and makes for the weeds near the bottom so stubbornly that, until I see where he is hooked, I try to persuade myself that I have at last got hold of a monster of the deep. The most productive spot is the end near the reeds, where a line of waterlily leaves are just showing. There I get one fish of nearly ¾ lb, beautifully shaped and marked, which really makes a determined struggle for liberty, actually reaching the weeds and for a moment attaching the dropper to one of them, which, fortunately, is not sufficiently firm to break the casting-line. And now for a few moments a change comes over the scene.

Hitherto there has been nothing but the lightest possible ripple, and often not even that; but now a sudden blast beats down from the hills, and the light boat is flying down the loch almost too rapidly for fishing, and, in spite of the utmost exertions of the man at the oars, the boat is down over the flies almost as soon as they touch the water. Two or three fish move at the fly in the course of the drift, but none of them are hooked, as it is really impossible to keep the line properly straight and strike in a workmanlike manner. It is but an easterly squall, and falls as rapidly as it rises; and, when a toiling and laborious pull up-wind has got us nearly back to the far end of the loch, all is calm once more, and rock, hill, and reed are reflected double in the glassy surface.

The basket at the end of the day contains only thirteen trout, and although there are one or two big ones, the average weight of the whole cannot be more than ¼ lb – a bad day both in number and size. At this time of the year I ought to be sure of at least a couple of dozen in an afternoon of about three to the pound. I

Loch fishing, evening coming in, photograph by John Tarlton

Salmon on the spawning grounds, by Robin Armstrong

have not changed my flies much, as the rising fish have seemed contented with what was offered them – a teal and green, a Zulu and an alder. My cast was a very fine one, and when for a short time I tried burn-trout flies of the smallest size on drawn gut, I did not meet with sufficient success to encourage me to persist in the experiment. I also condescended to a minnow for a short time while I enjoyed my after-luncheon pipe, but not a touch rewarded the poaching expedient. Altogether the pleasure of the day consisted rather in the delicious air, the beautiful landscape, and the life and music around me, than in the moderate sport enjoyed.

All day the birds have been busy and noisy, and I have noted fourteen varieties – herring-gull, kittiwake, heron, curlew, lapwing, sandpiper, duck, coot, moorhen, blackcock, grouse, rook, jackdaw, and cuckoo, without counting the smaller birds, such as swallows, martins, pipits, and warbler, the latter of which I find it difficult to identify with certainty at any distance.

I do not, of course, record the above day's sport as a typical or satisfactory sample of the pleasures of loch-fishing. I have had many days in various spots where the basket has been heavy at the end of the day, and fish up to 2 lb, with an occasional monster even larger, have rewarded my exertions. But just as marmalade has been described as 'an excellent substitute for butter at breakfast', so to my mind fishing in a loch from a boat is only a substitute for the real thing, and except for a change occasionally, I would rather have indifferent sport in a river or burn than fish the finest loch in the Highlands. I am far from saying that there is no skill in loch-fishing, or that knowledge of the locality, depth of water, and favourite haunts of big fish is not highly advantageous; but a few general rules, such as to prefer places where the water is only moderately deep, and be particularly attentive round sunken rocks, under overhanging boughs, near islands, or by patches of weeds, waterlilies, or reeds, will generally enable a stranger to a loch to make a good show at the end of the day if he understands the ordinary craft of the angler. Casting is never very difficult, as you drift along with the wind, and the temptation to a good fisherman to throw an unnecessarily long line is a stumbling-block and snare, except on the rare occasions when it enables him to cast over some rather distant fish he may have seen rise. To my mind, the most difficult thing in loch-fishing is to avoid entangling your line with that of some less expert brother angler who is casting from the same boat, and is erratic in his notions of time. A quick hand at the strike and unremitting observation and patience are of course essential for success. More skill is required in fishing from the shore or wading when a loch is thickly wooded, or the banks are approachable only from a few spots; but there are very few Scotch lochs where wading or bank-fishing give satisfactory results. Usually either the water deepens too rapidly, or reed beds or marshy deposit prevent your approaching the most likely spots.

This surely cannot be compared for sport to a ramble along some beautiful Highland stream, where the practised eye takes in the possibilities of every part of each successive reach or run. 'Chuck-and-chance-it fishing!' is the carping comment of the accomplished dry-fly trout-stalker of the south, to whose superior skill and mastery of the craft I bow with an awe and admiration entirely true and unfeigned. But although I may not have marked the three-pounder sucking down olive duns among the tresses, or seen the feeding fish lying near the surface, I must demur to the cynical description of my proceedings. Chuck I do, and chance it I must, to a certain extent; but there is all the difference in the world between the light and careless manner in which I rapidly move along some pebbly shallow or glassy reach, and the loving care with which I dwell upon the interstices among the rocks, the rippling, moderately strong runs, and other likely spots where instinct and experience tell me that trout are sure to rise. For sport and real fishing give me the riverbank, a clear stage, and no human companion, except perhaps at the midday lunch, until the close of the day.

But I am speaking of sport, and as a fisherman only. If I had not fished in lochs, I should have missed some of the most lovely scenes and enjoyable days I have ever spent. My mind recalls pictures of Loch Awe in the late spring, when the large globe ranunculus is in flower, of island, castle, rock, and wood, and Ben Cruachan towering overhead; of many a smaller tarn sparkling like a jewel among the hills; of the ospreys screaming over Loch Luichart, and of beautiful Colonsay with its three long lochs running straight in from the Atlantic, and Loch Sgoltaire among the hills higher up, with its ruined castle and lovely view of Mull through the cleft in the hills by the Cailleach. Perhaps it may be said that I might have seen all these lochs without fishing them. True enough, 0 sapient critic; but self-examination compels me to confess that it is most improbable that I should have done so.

A.E. Gathorne-Hardy, *Autumns in Argyleshire*
with Rod and Gun, 1900

Fishing in Lilliput

Not many of us can get fishing in such rivers as Test and Itchen where a pounder is a little fish. Nor can many of us fish regularly in such rivers as the Dove, the Eden and the Derbyshire Wye. We may get a day or two on such rivers in a season, but, for the most part, we have to make do with fishing less obviously good.

Happily, however, the pleasure of fishing is not strictly measurable in weight of fish, or in its annual cost, and some of the most delightful days are to be had on waters where anyone may fish who has a licence, closes gates, recognises that hedges are meant as barriers and not as sporting obstacles to be broken through, and never walks in unmown grass. These waters are of two kinds, those without any fish in them and those with many fish but small. These last, to those who know them, give some of the pleasantest fishing in the country. Sometimes, indeed, when the big rivers are out of order, many a man with the right to fish a nobler water has found himself well advised to leave that water and to go to fish in Lilliput instead.

In Lilliput everything is small, but the visiting fisherman remains, regretfully, his natural size. Small boys have an advantage in that country. Parts of the rivers in Lilliput are defended by bush and bramble which deter small boys much less than Gullivers. Other parts are so open that the man-mountain who would catch a fish there must be able to hide behind a molehill or a thistle. And, until he knows them, Gulliver is over-conscious of indignity in creeping so low to catch such little fish. For in the rivers of Lilliput the trout run small, from six to sixteen to the pound (some say thirty-two) though you will always meet a man who knew a man who hooked and lost a great fish that was 6 oz if it was a drachm. In Lilliput men who elsewhere jeer at an 8 in limit are inclined to complain of a 6 in limit as too big. Returning from Lilliput to the normal-sized world men find themselves excusing the little fish by saying that 'they eat very sweet'. So they do, but to say so is like finding that the best that can be said of a man is that 'he made a beautiful corpse'. The little fish of Lilliput deserve a handsomer obituary. Let me suggest a few of the praises that they earn. They are great fighters of their inches. There is almost no day on which they will not rise. When they rise, they rise heartily. Indeed they rise with such decision and promptitude that they ought to be both wealthy and wise. Very wise they are not. Wealthy? They are not in a rich country but in one where to keep a full stomach is riches, And they, by August, are plump as little alder-men and a great deal livelier.

The secret of getting the best out of fishing in Lilliput is to pretend that you are fishing in Brobdingnag. Attack a rising 3 oz fish as if you were trying to get a rise out of a three-pounder. It is

Anglers a-plenty, sketch by J.M.W. Turner

as difficult and therefore as interesting to float your dry fly past that diminutive nose as it is to offer it to a larger fish. You will probably get more fish with your three wet flies, but you will get more satisfaction out of a single dry one. The dry fly, even when taken by one of these hopo'-my-thumbs, requires a deliberation in the strike which gives to a rise an importance far greater than can ever be attributed to the sudden pluck and pull that make up the simultaneous rise and strike proper to the wet fly. Use a rod that will cast a short line and use the finest tackle you can get. Give yourself a chance of being broken by one of the rare ¼ lb veterans of the river. If you find you are getting too many fish, raise your size limit – by quarter inches. A careful adjustment of mind and tackle alike will give you days of as good fishing in Lilliput as ever you could get among the Brobdingnagian monsters. Disregard absolutely the advice of the books about fishing straight on if you fail to rise a fish that you have spotted. Make up your mind that if you choose to catch a particular fish of large size (say 7 in) you will catch him, if you have to smoke a pipe between each cast. Watch the fly on the water as if you were fishing for the epicures of the chalk streams. If the fish in Lilliput have a vice (which I do not like to admit), it is that they are too willing to take any fly you offer them. But even in Lilliput it will be found that on each day there is one fly that they will more willingly take than any other. If you make your own flies, you can be surer of appreciation in Lilliput than elsewhere, but here and there you will come across a little trout who rejects your fly and yet takes another the moment it has passed him. Such a trout is very valuable, no matter what his size, and when you outwit him by giving him just the fly he is preferring, he will set you up in your own mind for half a day.

My own favourite river in Lilliput is (but who gives away such secrets?) the…. It turns almost into a river of Brobdingnag before it reaches the sea, but that is many miles away. Tiny as it is, it is three rivers in one, providing three several sorts of fishing. One length of it, where the ¼ lb veterans lie, is in a deep gully, overhung with trees, almost dark at midday. Here, in the tunnel of green leaves, are short deep pools. You must wade if you are to get near the water at all and stoop if you are to get along under the boughs. There is no room for a 9 ft rod. This length is for the hottest days. Another length is fast, though much broken with Lilliput boulders. It invites the wet fly. (A greedy friend took six dozen trout from this length one day using three wet flies.) Even here a burly, bushy little dry fly is a pleasant sight dancing down the rapids and does, I think, take slightly bigger fish. The third length is the best. Its water is slow, with weeds instead of boulders. Its pools are very long, with a slowly smoothing surface below the runs. The only cover on either side of it is given by short rushes, each of which just now carries one of those little tufts which will not part with any fly that touches it. It is, in fact, a perfect length for dry fly fishing. The man who has fished up that short length and reached the top of it with, say, six fish and his temper well in hand has done something to be proud of. And, since the fish are Lilliput fish, he is not punished for his success by a heavy weight to carry as he walks back down the valley, the last of the sunlight on the mountains, the white scuts of the rabbits vanishing in the dusky fields and the first owls calling. In Lilliput no sunset is ever spoiled by the strap of a heavy basket insistently cutting the shoulder.

Arthur Ransome, *Rod and Line,* 1929

Pleasant Brooks and Store of Trout...

Piscator. Well, Scholer, now we are sate downe and are at ease, I shall tell you a little more of Trout fishing before I speak of the Salmon (which I purpose shall be next) and then of the Pike or Luce.

You are to know, there is night as well as day-fishing for a Trout, and that then the best are out of their holds; and the manner of taking them is on the top of the water with a great Lob or Garden worm, or rather two; which you are to fish for in a place where the water runs somewhat quietly (for in a stream it wil not be so well discerned). I say, in a quiet or dead place neer to some swift, there draw your bait over the top of the water to and fro, and if there be a good Trout in the hole, he will take it, especially if the night be dark; for then he lies boldly neer to the top of the water, watching the motion of any Frog or Water-mouse, or Rat betwixt him and the skie, which he hunts for if he sees the water but wrinkle or move in one of these dead holes, where the great Trouts usually lye neer to their hold.

And you must fish for him with a strong line, and not a little hook, and let

Portrait of Walton, by Arthur Rackham

him have time to gorge your hook, for he does not usually forsake it, as he oft will in the day-fishing: and if the night be not dark, then fish so with an Artificial fly of a light colour; nay he will sometimes rise at a dead Mouse or a piece of cloth, or any thing that seemes to swim cross the water, or to be in motion: this is a choice way, but I have not oft used it because it is void of the pleasures that such dayes as these that we now injoy, afford an Angler.

And you are to know, that in Hampshire, (which I think exceeds all England for pleasant Brooks, and store of Trouts) they use to catch Trouts in the night by the light of a Torch or straw, which when they have discovered, they strike with a Trout spear; this kind of way they catch many, but I would not believe it till I was an eye-witness of it, nor like it now I have seen it.

Izaak Walton,
The Compleat Angler, 1653

Spinner Time

It was on the edge of spinner time that I came out after tea on an August Saturday afternoon and made my way up the east bank of the Itchen to a bend which runs almost due west to east, where it was my purpose to await the early stages of the evening rise. I had hardly 'attained my objective', when I marked a rise at the tail of a bunch of cut weed which was bunched against my own bank. It was a soft rise, but definite enough; but I was too near.

Dropping cautiously into the tall reeds and willowherb, I retreated a few paces, and thence I delivered my seal's fur-bodied red spinner to the address. It fell a couple of feet further into the stream than I intended, but it was of no consequence, for the fly had not travelled a foot before my rod was bending to the plunge of a grayling whose inches indicated a weight of close on 2 lb. He was in due course conducted ashore, and was followed by a brace of his fellows of about 1 lb each out of the next three rises spotted on the same length. It looked as if the evening was going to prove a soft thing for me. But it is never safe to count on the willingness of grayling as any clue to the disposition of the trout, or vice versa.

By the time I had reached the bend (and the reach was little more than 100 yd long) I had seen no other rise, and the weather, which for four and twenty days had been blazing, began to show definite signs of breaking up. The wind, however, what little there was, came from the south-east, and I thought there would be little beyond a spit,

and that soon over. So I pushed my way through the masses of willowherb, often topping my head by a foot or two, and made for the first gap at which I might hope to find the river accessible.

As luck would have it, I came out at a spot where the weeds were growing out of the river for eight or ten yards from the bank. On the outer edge lay a trout something better than a pound, obviously waiting for the rise to begin. I offered him the spinner, and it fell just beyond and behind him. He turned languidly, followed it down for a couple of yards, then opened his mouth as if to take it, thought better of it, and returned to his station. Of a second offer he took no notice, so I decided to try him with a sedge of small size. When, however, I looked up from knotting on my fly, he was gone. The rain, however, was not. Still, it was not heavy, and I decided to push on. Yet, by way of precaution, before

Fishing the shallows, by John Reid

John R Reid

Battling a salmon, by Ernest Briggs

pushing through more masses of willowherb, I decided to slip on my light mackintosh, and soon had reason to be glad I had done so. For no sooner was I definitely committed to that eastern bank, with acres of marsh and bog between me and real dry land, than the rain began to come down with a will. I took it, however, in good part, for my waders protected my legs and my mackintosh my body, and only my hat took a soaking.

When I started along that bank, however, I had little notion how the tall growths cut one off from access to the river, and how little of it was fishable from that side with a nine-footer. Here and there I saw an occasional rise under the western bank where the current set but, generally speaking, I was cut off by the growth on the bank from casting to most of the fish, and the three which I did succeed in covering in the next half-mile would have nothing to do with me. Then I reached a more open bend with the current under my own bank. Here I found a couple of grayling dimpling, but they would have no truck with me. My gauze net showed that some black gnats were going down; also a little dark spinner, and an occasional sedge. I put up a little dark rusty spinner in the hope of finding a trout in one of the familiar corners in an accommodating humour but there was none moving, and I was again committed to battle with the marsh herbage, and by the time I arrived at the choice length where the current ran deep under my own bank, my mackintosh was as wet with sweat inside as with rain from the willowherb, the sedges and the reeds on the outside, and still I was troutless. To add to my discomfiture, the wind, instead of dying down, as it should have done, began to get up, and soon was blowing briskly from the south, bringing with it torrents of rain, which my light mackintosh was not sufficient entirely to repel, and I began to feel an unpleasant sensation of cold in my elbows. Gladly would I have gone in, but it was still three-quarters of an hour to the time when the keeper was due at the opposite bank to punt over and fetch me. There was nothing for it but to stick it out. But here again I found the rain-laden willowherb higher and denser than ever, and I had to push through masses of it before I could get a sight of the river at all.

At length I came to a place where the growth was different and reached little above my waist, and here I stood in the rain for the best part of half an hour while the dark made rapid progress. The trend of the river here was from north-east to south-west, and under my bank there was thus a little shelter from the wind.

Presently the rain thinned to a drizzle and I became aware of something that looked like a recurring heavy drip in the water under my bank. There was nothing to drip from, however, and, watching, I made up my mind that it was a trout and that it was taking spinners. How I tied on an orange seal's-fur (sherry) spinner in that light with my hat pouring torrents over my hands I do not know, but I made a sound job of it. Seven, eight, or nine times I covered the trout with a line not seven yards long from the tip of my rod, and then there was a sudden jar as a most indignant trout took the point in the extreme tip of his lip. He tore almost all my line off in the first rush. I could not follow him, as I did not want to disturb what was left to me of open bank, so I had to let him run. But presently I had him back under the rod point and dished him out – 1 lb 10 oz.

Meanwhile, the rain had ceased and a curious threatening glare showed upon the sky and reflected on the surface. It enabled me to detect another quiet dimple almost on the edge of the ruffled water. One offer was enough. I struck at the dimple and felt a hard jar: a good fish sprang wildly into the air, and my line came back to me. There was not another twenty yards of open bank left to me, and I was determined not to commit myself to further battle with the willowherb. So I watched carefully and, peering into the dusk, made out just one other riser under my own bank. The spinner was his game, too, and presently he took his place in my bag, adding 1 lb 3 oz to the burden on my shoulders, but taking quite that weight off my spirits. There was nothing more to be seen moving, so I reeled up and started to force my way back through a couple of yards to the place where the keeper was waiting with the punt to ferry me over to land that was land, and a short way back to my inn. And as I crouched drenched in the slushing punt I reflected that things had come about differently from my anticipation, and that it was not the evening, but I that had turned out to be a soft thing.

G.E.M. Skues *Itchen Memories*, 1951

Larger than Life

Big fish, really big fish, larger fish than you've ever seen before – except on someone else's wall or in a garish photograph – provide electric excitement, a sudden quick challenge to all you have learned in your marrowbones, and a relief from smaller fare. And just as surely, they are a lure that hooks you to fish more. For something bigger. For a record perhaps. For a fish that has some claim to immortality. Which can be a serious business.

I know people – young and old – who live for such outsized fish. One cock of the walk is interested only in the biggest salmon. He is a big-fish fisherman of the first water. He's also a big fish in the art pool in which he swims and he only wants to catch big fish there, too. His talk is a litany of accomplishments; he always wants the newest, biggest, best, most; he does not 'pick up a pen' for less than several hundred thousand dollars. And he generally gets the newest, biggest, best, most, which he needs, which back his advertisements for himself. He wants records and mounts; he is bored with less.

I would be too often dissatisfied if that's all I came to fly fish for – the big fish. Dreams would too often outrun reality. But there is more to those big fish, something not pathological. They nibble at my brain – albeit they're usually the fish that have gotten away.

They stretch us, expand the circle that contains our sense of ourselves, the limits of some imaginative construction of what we can and cannot do. Roger Bannister spent years trying to break the barrier of the four-minute mile and then dozens did it; many fishermen catch permit regularly on the fly, though this was once rare; and more fly fishers hold larger trout than they dreamed could be held on a No. 20 dry fly. Big fish jolt us. They are bigger than life, or make life bigger. They swim in our brains for decades, long after lesser fare have faded – bigger, older, rarer, more difficult, unusual, commanding our hardest-won respect.

Nick Lyons, *Spring Creek*, 1992

One to go back, by Tom Quinn of a barbel taken on a fly

Halford meets Skues

We had heard on the day of our arrival in Winchester that the great man was putting up at The George and was nightly welcoming his worshippers at that hotel to hear him expound the pure and authentic gospel of the dry fly – which no one would dream of questioning. So that evening found us, after our meal, among the humble listeners. It came to our ears on that occasion that we were to have the great man's company on the Abbots Barton water, the lessee having invited him for a week.

With becoming reverence we listened to his words of wisdom until it became necessary that the session be broken up. On the following day we were on the water a quarter of an hour or so before our mentor's arrival – taking the side stream, my friend above in the Ducks' Nest Spinney, I a couple of hundred yards further downstream, thus leaving the main river, the fishing of which was reputed the better, to the great man. He was not long behind us and presently we saw him casting on Winnel Water, the main river. Soon afterwards he crossed the meadow which divided the two streams and accosted me from the left bank of the side stream to advise us kindly on the fly to put up, and to make his advice clearer he cast his fly on the right bank of the side stream, having first ascertained that I had mounted a fly of George Holland's dressing, known as the quill

marryat. He insisted that his fly, which was an India-rubber olive, was the right fly. My selection was based on little pale duns seen on the water. I took a look at his fly and was not a little shocked to see how coarse was the gut on which his fly was tied, but I was also too polite or timid to venture on such a comment.

We met at lunch-time and he inquired how I had done. I said two and a half brace. He had one trout only, but congratulated me civilly and offered to put me up for the Flyfishers' Club, then recently formed. Not expecting, despite my additional thirteen pounds in ten days, to live long enough to make it worthwhile, I declined and did not in fact seek membership till the autumn of 1893, when a voyage to the Cape and back had gone a long way to re-establishing my health.

F.M. Halford, from an anonymous painting

Halford only fished the Abbots Barton length for three more days of his week, but just as I had been profoundly shocked to do better than the great master did on the first day, I was fared to be similarly shocked on each of his three other days. Yet it encouraged me to rely most on my own observations and not to attach undue importance to authority. My friend, by the way, caught the biggest fish of the week (one pound thirteen ounces), but it was his only catch.

G.E.M. Skues, *Itchen Memories,* 1951

London's Rivers

The London Angler has but seldom the pleasure of bringing home a dish of Trout caught in either the river Thames or Lea; for those rivers, however famous they may have been, at present contain very few, but those are very large and fat, some weighing more than ten pounds.

There are, certainly, many good Trout streams within twenty miles of the metropolis, but they are all private property. Yet here the gentlemen Angler is seldom refused a day's fair fishing. The river Wandle, particularly at Carshalton, in Surrey, has numerous fine Trout; and again, at Merton-mills, &c., till you arrive at Wandsworth, and is the best and clearest stream near London for Trout. The little river called Ravensbourn, running from or by Sydenham, Lewisham, &c., to the Kent-road, Greenwich, has Trout; also the Darent, or Dartford-creek, may boast of very fine Trout; and at Crayford, Bexley,

An illustration from Dame Juliana Berners', *A Treatyse of Fysshynge Wyth an Angle,* 1496

Foot's Cray, Paul's Cray, &c., and near the powder mills, through and near Darent, and Horton, to Farningham, in Kent; also near Hertford, in the water belonging to Earl Cowper, Mr Baker, and other gentlemen; and at Wade's-mill; and in the river Colne, near St Alban's; and at Whet Hampstead, &c. At Rickmansworth and Watford, in Hertfordshire, and its neighbourhood, are several good Trout stream and from thence to Uxbridge, in Middlesex; at the latter place, the Angler may indulge himself in angling for Trout, by paying for board and lodging, at the Crown and Cushion, or at the White Horse inns.

T.F. Salter, *The Anglers Guide,* 1833

Forty winks, anonymous line drawing, 19th century

Mayfly Time

Those who fish rivers where Mayfly come will agree that, though with it you get a higher average weight, yet actually the biggest fish are killed on the sedge. 1903 on the Kennet was a great mayfly season for heavy fish, and a friend of mine who had the Ramsbury water got the truly remarkable bag of six fish in one day which weighed over nineteen pounds: and yet the two heaviest fish of the year were got on the sedge.

I got the heaviest. It was 26 July, a cloudy, gusty day, with a downstream wind, and I was on the water from eleven till five without seeing a rise. My friend and I then had tea and walked up the river at a quarter past six. Olives began to appear and trout to move; and suddenly a really large one started rising. We stood and watched, with growing excitement. He was taking every fly, in solid and determined fashion, and the oftener he appeared the bigger he looked, and the faster beat our hearts. It was settled that I was to try for him. I was nervous and uncomfortable. He was very big: it was a long throw and the wind horrible: I could not reach him, and like a fool I got rattled and pulled off too much line: there was an agonised groan from my friend behind me when a great curl of it was slapped on the water exactly over the trout's nose. We looked at each other without speaking, and he silently walked away up the river, leaving me staring stupidly at the spot where the trout had been rising. Of course he was gone.

The next two hours can be passed over. The small fly rise came and went. I caught a trout on a No. 2 silver sedge and finally, at about a quarter past eight, found myself gazing gloomily at the place where I had bungled. The wild wind had blown itself out and had swept the sky bare of cloud. Silence had come, and stillness. The willows, which all through the long summer day had bowed and chattered in the wind, were straightened and motionless, each individual leaf hanging down as though carved in jade: the forest of great sedges, which the gusts had swept into wave after wave of a roaring sea of emerald, was now calm and level, each stalk standing straight and stiff as on a Japanese screen. There had occurred that transition, that transmutation from noise and movement to silence and peace, which would be more wonderful were we not so accustomed to it, when a windy summer day turns over to a moveless summer night: when the swing and clatter and rush of the day is arrested and lifted from the world, and you get

Brown trout, by Neil Dalrymple

the sense that the great hollow of the air is filled with stillness and quiet, as with a tangible presence.

They are peaceful things, these summer evenings after wild days, and I remember particularly that this was one of the most peaceful; more so indeed than my thoughts, which were still in a turmoil. I stood watching mechanically, and then, tempting fate to help me, made a cast or two over the spot where the fish had been. How easy it was to reach it now, how lightly my fly settled on the water, how gracefully it swung over the place. All to no purpose,

of course, for nothing happened, and I was about to reel up when a fish rose ten yards above, close under my bank. It was one of those small movements difficult to place. It might be a very large fish or a very small one. A wild thought swept through me that this was my big one: but no, I said to myself, it cannot be. This is not where he was rising. Besides, things do not happen like that, except in books: it is only in books that you make a fearful bungle and go back later and see a small break which you think is a dace, and cast carelessly and hook something the size of an autumn salmon: it is only in books that fate works in such fashion. Why, I know it all so well that I could write it out by heart, every move of it. But this is myself by a river, not reading in a chair. This is the real world, where such things do not happen: that is the rise of a half-pound trout.

I cast. I was looking right into the west, and the water was coloured like skimmed milk by reflection from where the sun had set. My silver sedge was as visible as by day. It floated down, there was a rise, I struck, and something rushed upstream. Then I knew. Above me was open water for some twenty-five yards, and above that again a solid block of weed, stretching right across. My fish made for this, by short, irresistible runs. To let him get into it would have been folly: he must be stopped: either he is well hooked or lightly, the gut is either sound or rotten: kill or cure, he must be turned, if turned he can be: so I pulled hard, and fortunately got his head round and led him down. He played deep and heavy and I had to handle him roughly, but I brought him down with a smash, and I began to breathe again. But then another terror appeared. In the place we had reached the only clear water was a channel under my bank, and the rest of the river was choked with weed.

Should I try to pull him down this channel, about three or four yards wide, to the open water below? No. It was much too dangerous, for the fish was uncontrollable, and if he really wanted to get to weed he would either get there or break me: even with a beaten fish it would be extremely risky, and with an unbeaten one it was unthinkable. Well, if he would not come down he must go up, and up he went willingly enough, for when I released pressure he made a long rush up to the higher weed bed, whilst I ran up the meadow after him, and with even greater difficulty turned him once more. This time I thought he was really going right through it, so fast and so heavy was his pull, and I think he was making for a hatch hole above: but once more my gallant gut stood the strain and, resisting vigorously, he was led down again. This proceeding was repeated either two or three times more, I forget which: either three or four times we fought up and down that twenty-five yards of river.

By then he was tiring, and I took up my station in the middle of the stretch, where I hoped to bring him in: my hand was actually on the sling of the net when he suddenly awoke and rushed up. He reached the weed bed at a pace at which it was impossible to stop, shot into it like a torpedo, and I had the sickening certainty that I should lose him after all. To hold him hard now would be to make a smash certain, so I slacked off: when he stopped I tightened again, expecting miserably to feel the dead, lifeless drag of a weeded line. Instead, to my delight, I found I was still in contact with the fish, and he was pulling hard. How he had carried the line through the weeds I do not know. To look at it seemed impossible … But the line was clear, and the fish proved it by careering wildly on towards the hatch, making the reel sing. I believe he meant to go through into the carrier, as fish have done before and after, but I turned him. However, we could not stay where we were.

The hatch was open at the bottom, there was a strong draw of water through it, and if a heavy, beaten fish got into this, no gut would hold him up. At all risks he must be taken over the weed into the clear water. I pulled him up to the top and ran him down. Then, for the first time after so many perils, came the conviction that I should land him. He was obviously big, but how big could not be known, for I had not had a clear sight of him yet. He still pulled with that immovable, quivering solidity only shown by a very heavy fish. But at last even his great strength tired. He gave a wobble or two, yielded and suddenly he was splashing on the top, looking huge in the dusk.

There ensued that agonising time when you have a big fish nearly beat, but he is still too heavy to pull in, and nothing you can do gets him up to the net. At last I pulled him over to it, but I lifted too soon, the ring caught in the middle of the body, he wavered a moment in the air and then toppled back into the water with a sickening splash. A judgment, I thought, and for a shattering second I believed he had broken the gut, but he was still on. I was pretty well rattled by then and, in the half light, made two more bad shots, but the end came at last, he was in the net and on the bank.

How big was he? Three pounds? Yes, and more. Four pounds? Yes, and more. Five? He might be, he might. My knees shook and my fingers trembled as I got him on the hook of the steelyard. He weighed a fraction over four pounds eight ounces.

J.W. Hills, *A Summer on the Test*, 1924

North Country

It was towards the fag end of the Mayfly season – the second Saturday in June, to be correct – that a Leeds expert accompanied me to a little village a few miles from Helmsley on the Rye, our avowed intention being to give the trout a thorough plating.

Unfortunately, the day of our choice turned out a miserable, cold and forbidding affair, just like the yesterday and the day before, and looking in vain for a rise of that most delicately beautiful of all nature's insect efforts – the diaphanous-winged green drake – we descended basely from our proud pedestal and were reduced to catching minnows to use as an alternative lure. For a time the fish were every whit as dour as the day, and gave but a negative indication that they were engaged in the serious occupation of pushing each other out of the way to get at the bait. Then, for some unaccountable reason, they suddenly wakened up and at almost every cast there was a savage little grab.

Five or six nice trout were quickly creeled, and then I found myself at the top of a broad corner. Now this particular spot was specially interesting to me, for the landlord at the little hostelry – where my companion, being an enthusiastic motorist, had persuaded me to call to lubricate the interchangeables – had whispered in my ear that a village expert had been 'broken to blazes' there only the day before by a fish anything up to a yard long, which had retained his fly and a length of gut as a souvenir. I decided, therefore, to spin every inch of it carefully and thoroughly.

The first cast had scarcely been half fished through when there was a decided drag, and I felt that I was at least into something good. Not knowing exactly the strength of the opposition, I gave him his head and allowed him as much latitude – and longitude – as he desired, and in a few minutes slipped the net under – not a yard of trout certainly, but a nice enough fish, which subsequently balanced a pound weight exactly. Well now, I know you'll not believe it, but firmly fixed in its upper jaw was a strawbodied artificial May, with about five inches of gut attached. And such gut! It was of the undrawn grade, and would have made short work of lifting five or six pounds dead weight. Of course, I called to my friend, who was not far away, to witness the proceeding. 'Now,' said he, 'just you lend me that fly and we'll have some fun when we get back to the Bug and Gluepot' – which we did, but more of that anon.

This was to be a day of extraordinaries, apparently, for at the very next cast I hooked something which went off like a streak of lightning and resisted all attempts at breaking for at least twenty yards. I shouted lustily that the other fish was a counterfeit, and that I was securely moored to the 'whopper'. My brother piscator came up at a run to see the fun, and was not disappointed, for he put

up a rare fight for several minutes, then suddenly caved in and was brought to view – a twelve-ounce fish hooked by the tail! This accounted, of course, for his strenuous but unavailed bid for liberty.

When we arrived back at headquarters the first person we met was the gent who had lost the 'plugger'. My friend tipped me a wink – what for I did not know – and slid off in a hurry to find mine host. In a minute or two the latter strolled to the door and, addressing the local, intimated that the gentleman inside had caught the fish he had lost the day before. 'Ah shud think he'll be very neer fower,' he observed, and never moved a muscle. 'The devil he will!' was the reply. 'Where is un?'

We went to see, and there on the table, with half-a-dozen grinning yokels grouped around, lay a little troutlet into the mouth of which the rescued fly had been deftly introduced. 'Where's t'fish?' enquired the excited native. 'There,' said the smiling landlord, pointing to the fingerling. 'Ah told yer 'e wor neerly fower ounces.' Considerable argument ensued, and just as things were getting quite pleasantly warm, the two strangers from Leeds slipped away and reached the station just in time to board the 'slow', en route for the West Riding. But the native got his own back with interest, for the next time we wrote for permission we were politely refused by the owner, and just as politely informed that he objected to permitees retaining small fish!

J.H.R. Bazeley, *Fishing Stunts*, 1916

Fishing the River Gade, photograph by Richard Smith

Pea-shooter

He was an old and wise fish, and had his headquarters opposite a clubhouse on a certain famous stream. Many a fly had passed over his venerable head. Once long ago it is said that he was hooked on a piece of bread, but quickly wound the line round a stump, extracted the hook and was rising to some natural flies half an hour later. New members used to bet that they would catch him. The old members took their bets and their money and obtained satisfaction out of the fish that way. It was an aggravating feature in that trout's behaviour that nothing would put him down short of a cart rope thrown over his head. He was as tame as a pug dog, but had the cunning, without the wildness, of a hawk.

One day there joined the club a man who was not an expert with the fly rod. He, like the rest, said he thought he could catch the trout. The old members laughed and took his bets, as was their custom with newcomers. A mean thing this, but very much the way of the world.

It was August. One sultry evening the new member came to the club armed with a pea-shooter and many bluebottles. Was he going to catch the trout with a pea-shooter? No; he was only going to begin to catch him – the operation might take some time. Deftly a half-dead bluebottle was puffed out of the tube in front of the fish.

It was taken, of course, as everything eatable from a trout's point of view was taken. The fish had a rare supper that evening.

The following day the new member repeated the operation. He fed the fish in this manner for more than a week; the others smiled and looked on. 'I will catch him soon,' said the new member. 'I am only waiting for wind.'

At the end of three weeks there came a day when a stiff breeze was blowing upstream. It was the day on which the catastrophe

On the fly, by A. Rowland Knight

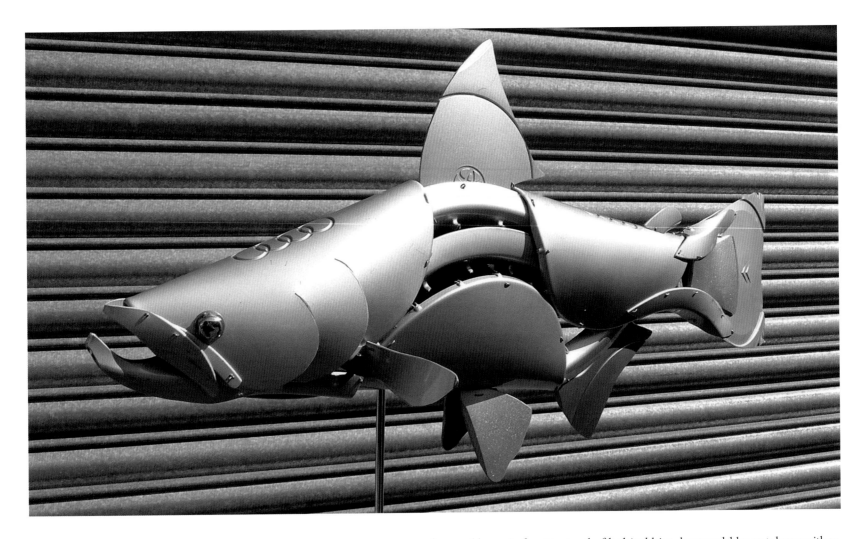

Hubcap fish, by Ptolemy Elrington

was fated to happen. The new member appeared at the clubhouse with a long slender rod, on which was arranged running tackle and a length of fine but strong gut, terminating with a single hook.

He took his stand some distance below the fish, and began feeding him as usual. On the hook was a bluebottle. Good luck helped our friend who, however, exhibited considerable skill. The upstream breeze took the hooked fly just over the trout, and the new member let it fall and at the same time puffed out a fly from the tube.

Which would the trout take? It was an anxious moment. Had the

rod been in front instead of behind him, he would have taken neither. But he did not see the rod, having no eyes in his tail (this has been questioned) and the fly containing the hook was sucked in.

How he fought! Was the wisdom of twenty years to culminate in destruction by means of a pea-shooter and a bluebottle? Where was that invaluable stump? The new member had removed it. The weeds? They had been recently cut. A leap for liberty then? That made matters worse for the gut got wound round his body and hampered him sadly. But let fall the curtain. He died – as wise and grand and noble a specimen as has ever been seen in a trout stream.

John Bickerdyke, *Days of My Life,* 1895

Not as Big as You Think

To the end of one's angling life, I suppose, one will continue at times to be misled by the appearance of things, and of fish among them. Every season I get an occasional disappointment on catching some trout which, seen at a distance, had struck me as being beyond the common in point of size. But a short time ago I had a rather ignominious experience of the kind.

In a tiny stream in which I had acquired angling rights, though circumstances had prevented me from making much use of them, I discovered a red trout lying at the point where the water, from being a system of two or three nothings making damp threads through a meadow, concentrates itself into a single channel and is recognisable as a brook. There is, in fact, a little pool at this point, and in this pool I could see two or three trout, particularly the big red one.

He looked very impressive in so small a place, and I unhesitatingly estimated him at two and a half pounds, which would be a huge fish for the water, whose average weight is more like ten ounces. And I was confirmed in my opinion when after taking my Wickham's Fancy he bolted downstream into a clump of rushes, and smashed my cast as if it had been cobweb. Worse than this, I confided my opinion to one or two others who might be interested in the matter, and committed myself to the story that the brook held trout up to two and a half pounds. That sort of story gives a fishery dignity and importance.

I only had one more day's fishing there before the season closed, and then I was unfortunate enough to catch, among others, my red trout, whom I found lying in exactly the same place and on whom I tried forcing tactics as soon as I had hooked him, on a cocliybonddu this time. I found the forcing tactics unexpectedly successful, the reason being clear when the fish came to the spring balance and made no more than one pound five ounces. Seldom have I been worse deceived by a fish; I suppose the confined space in which he had his abode made him seem disproportionately big. Fortunately on the same day I discovered another trout in a little hatch-hole which enabled me to stick to the 'up to two and a half pounds' account. His head and shoulders must have weighed that, though I question whether the rest of him weighed anything. He was a lamentable twenty inches of trout. I fully expected to catch him when I saw what he was like (though as a matter of fact I did not), for the reason that if there is a decrepit fish anywhere about which only weighs half what it should, it is almost certain to come and take my fly. Possibly my fondness for fishing in odd places, backwaters, carriers, millheads, and the like, lays me open to this, for bad old fish certainly tend to inhabit the quieter and less vigorous parts of a water. Even the well-known monster which lies under a bridge often turns out to be mostly head, and presumably he has some easy nook behind a buttress or in an eddy where he can avoid the exertion of constantly breasting a strong stream. You do not often catch one of these bridge trout, and when you do it almost always disappoints you by not coming up to your expectations of its weight.

One of my most grievous disappointments I have related elsewhere. I marked a great trout feeding in a portion of the Kennet and Avon canal, succeeded in getting him to take a dry Wickham, and for several minutes was convinced that I had on the fish of my dry-fly career. It proved indeed to be about twenty-four inches long when at last I got him out, but unfortunately he was one of the old breed which has become dolefully familiar to me, and instead of weighing a good seven pounds as he should have, he only touched four and a half pounds. In the water, of course, he seemed much more than that owing to his great length, and as I was using fine gut the fight was long enough to have been put up by a six or seven-pounder.

As a matter of fact I have only once caught a bigger fish with dry fly, and that was at Blagdon, so it could scarcely claim special honours. It was satisfactory, however, as rewarding a real bit of dry-fly work. I found the fish rising late in the evening in the river at the Butcombe Bay end (the lake was low that summer, so there was a good deal of river in evidence) covered it with a sedge just as if it had been a Kennet fish, and landed it after a real hard fight, four and three-quarter pounds. I remember the clock striking ten as I lifted it out in my landing-net.

This was a fish of reasonable shape and solidity, but rainbows are rather apt to be disappointing on the scales because of their short life and their tendency to deteriorate at an age when brown trout would still be putting on ounces. I caught one once at Ravensthorpe Reservoir, the lake which is famous as one of the

Deep wading, by Joseph Crawhall

early proofs of what results can be got from trout culture in water storage lakes, which was rising just like that Blagdon fish, with heavy deliberation suggestive of great size. And it was a big fish, or rather it had been once. It was shaped more like an eel than a trout, and, even so, it weighed two and a half pounds. I have no doubt that in happier days it had been at least twice as heavy.

But, as I have said, it has been my luck to meet with that sort of fish very frequently, so an instance more or less no longer surprises me. I could wish that I was less favoured with regard to big ones of that type.

I do not remember ever hooking and losing the sort of trout that makes history, or at any rate the sort of trout that I honestly believed would have made history. I am not exempt, of course, from the common fisherman's failing of estimating 'the big one that got away' on a perhaps too generous scale. The biggest trout that I ever hooked, of which I am certain, I was fortunate enough to land. It came from the famous weirpool at Uxbridge and weighed two ounces under eight pounds. It took a dilapidated metal spinning bait of the Devon type and gave me a great fight. I had

at that time never seen a trout out of the water of anything like such a size, and I had no idea what it would weigh. Five pounds was as much as I dared to hope for, so my pride and joy when the scales at the keeper's cottage revealed the truth can be imagined. It was a beautiful fish twenty-five inches long and with deep, gleaming flanks, a picture of an old Colne trout. I had other good and handsome fish from that pool and the stream below afterwards, but nothing to approach that one. The biggest was four and a half pounds. Another angler a few years later got one of seven and a quarter pounds. The Colne has in its time yielded a good many fish of about that size, but I am afraid that some parts of it have now seen their best days. The extraordinary catches at West Drayton made during the years when the water was heavily stocked with big fish, suggest that the river may yet be capable of recovery. The fish seem to thrive well enough in its lower reaches, though of course the Thorney Weir records are not due to the natural breeding capacities of the stream.

H.T. Sheringham, *Trout Fishing Memories and Morals*, 1920

On the Wylye

About this time I started making my own rods and I have to this day a 12 ft rod, with an ash butt, hickory middle, and greenheart tops. This rod killed me many trout; for I had not forgotten what I had learnt at Winchester. I used this rod for several years, when I gave it up in favour of a two-jointed 11 ft greenheart I had made.

In those days we had not nearly so many flies as the fisherman has today. There were the duns, the quills, the palmers, the spinners, haresear, cowdung, and the alder. This latter fly I have always considered the last hope of the dry-fly fisherman, but few now try it. Often when all else has failed I have known it successful. It has, though, I always thought, a great fault; it is not tied on a hook with a wide enough bend; the body of peacock harl is bulky, and often one does not get enough hold, and one is, in consequence, likely to lose fish.

One very hot cloudless day in June, when I could find nothing doing, I saw a fish rise under a horse chestnut tree in the garden of Norton Bavant Manor House. This fish could not be got at from where I was, and my 11 ft rod was too long to work under the tree from the other side. So I walked back to Bishopstrow, eating my lunch as I went. I put away the 11 ft rod, and sallied out again with a little 8 ft one. I went into the garden where I had leave to go and sure enough the trout was still rising under the tree in the shade. He took an alder at once, and I proceeded to land him,

when to my horror he went through the bottom of my net, which was rotten. I held the net up the line, and fortunately he was well hooked, so I was able to net him once more, telling him to try to go through again. It was not a big trout but one of about ½ to 1 lb. I then tied up the net as well as I could, and looked up and down the river under the trees. It was not long before I saw another trout rise. I waited until he came up again, and then put the alder over him, which he took at once. I got this one out; he was about the same size. I was then done as I could not spot another. I therefore walked downstream to where there was a willow-bed island. I knew here there would be sixty or seventy yards of shade. At once I saw two rises. I watched the lower one of the two for a bit, and when I saw he was on the feed I tried him, with the same result; I also killed the other. So ended my day – four trout 5½ lb.

The limit on the Wylye was 1 lb – we returned all fish under this weight. The trout in the river were game fish, but did not eat well, as they were mostly muddy. We were not altogether dry-fly purists in those days; if it was a rough, blowy day, or a wet one, we often used the wet fly, and often with good results.

One Saturday afternoon I went to a tennis party from which I returned some half-hour before it was necessary to dress for dinner. As a rule we avoided Saturday evening for fishing, because the farmers used to flood the meadows on these afternoons, which upset the river; but as it was a beautiful evening I picked up my

Fishing scene from the Manesse illuminated manuscript (1340)

rod and walked across a small meadow with my flannel trousers rolled up to my knees. My objective was the next meadow. The grass was some six or eight inches high, and was wet with the flooding; and I got half-way across when I trod on an eel of 2 to 3 lb. The brute coiled round my bare leg, and I do not think I ever jumped and kicked so much in my life: it was the most terrible feeling I ever experienced. It was many seconds before I could free my leg, and when I did I turned and ran home as hard as I could. No more fishing for me that night.

I once had a curious fight with one of these gentry in the Pill Hole of Bishopstrow Mill, at about 10 p.m. The big trout there used to drop back into the shallow at the tail of the pool in the evening, and one could often get one with a large March brown. One night, it being nearly dark, as it would be at 10 p.m., I was trying for a fish rising there when I hooked a big eel by the middle as I was lifting the line from the water. This gentleman went round the pool, which was a big one, in right earnest, and it was not until about a quarter of an hour after, when it was pitch dark, that I got on terms with him. I was standing in about a foot of water, which I suppose did not help matters. When I got his head in the net his tail came out, and when I got his tail in the net his head came out. This happened several times, and finally he got up into the deep water again and broke me. I once did the same thing in a Scotch loch, but it was in the daytime, and I landed one of 2½ lb.

I used to notice a thing on the Wylye that I have never been able to explain. Above the mills on the river there was always a long, still, deep stretch of water. These places were often very good water, and held big trout; but if the miller shut down his hatches to get up a head of water it always stopped the rise, no matter what amount of fly was on the water. There was one of these stretches of dead water above Norton Bavant Mill, and in the evening the fish rose well there; but so still was the water (it had almost an oily look, though it was quite pure) that it was useless to try these fish upstream, even with the finest of gut. There was only one chance of getting hold of them, and it was a slender chance, as one only had one cast. What one used to do was to

Trout and eels, by John Singer Sargent

approach the river on one's stomach from above, and if one could put the fly about three inches above where the trout rose one had him for a certainty. But if one made a bad shot the game was up.

In those days I was young and active, also I did not mind getting wet, and I wore no waders. One day I was standing with a great friend on the road bridge over the Wylye between Sutton Veney and the Heytesbury Road. We were eating our lunch at the time, looking downstream. Just below us was a large patch of weed with a narrow channel up the middle of it, and in this channel was a trout who took no notice of us, but kept on rising as if we were not there. He was about fifteen yards off and I suppose he was accustomed to seeing people on the bridge. I said to my friend, 'See me hook that fellow down there.'

Said he, 'I will bet you twopence you don't from here.'

Whereupon I put an olive down just above his nose, which he took at once and promptly ran into the weeds. I put my left hand on the parapet of the bridge and vaulted over, landing in some three feet of water, to the surprise and somewhat to the horror of a party of ladies who were driving past in a trap. Having landed in the river safely, I walked down the channel to just above where my trout was, and then proceeded to tread him out of the weeds. This did not take long to do, and I landed him just below. Now, in those days of youth and exuberant activity the jump into the river seemed nothing to me, but some three years ago I was motoring past the place, and in fact, eating my lunch on the same bridge, and I inspected the site of my jump. To my eyes it seemed to be a very much bigger drop than I had remembered it to be, and I would not do it now for any trout, however big he might be.

H. Langford Brown, *By the Water's Side*, 1936

Salmon

A Day with the Grilse

It is one of the wettest mornings of this very wet autumn of the year of grace 1890. The keeper has reported in the gun-room, on being asked whether it was any good to go out on the hill, that 'the dry land was over your boots', and that the birds would be quite unapproachable.

Still, the glass is rising at last, and although the water has been too high to begin with yesterday and the day before, and has committed on each day the unpardonable sin of rising and flooding us out when fishing, I determine to go again to the river for two reasons: (1) the day is wholly unsuitable for any other sport or amusement; (2) I know that there are fish in the river, and this heavy flood, just as the nets are off at the mouth, with a spring-tide at its highest, must have brought in others. Besides, it has rained so much that it surely cannot rain any more; the stock must be exhausted; and lastly, if other reasons are wanting, a true fisherman requires a great deal to keep him at home. After all, the rain that fell last night can have been nothing but a mist, although it splashed round the house like a shower-bath – or, at least, it must have been less on the hills at the sources of the Add – so the dog-cart is duly ordered to be at the door at 10.30. My wife, after vainly expostulating, suggests that I should put on a pair of shooting-boots instead of waders, so that 'if I should have a gleam of sanity I can walk home. Surely, at any rate, I will not take the child with me?' But, the child, an embryo schoolboy of nine, and myself, being of a different opinion, the majority of voices carry the day; and at the hour fixed for starting we both mount the dog-cart in high glee, fully persuaded that, although the rain is still falling, it really is the clearing shower which has been prophesied for the last six weeks and has arrived at last.

Faith is rewarded this time. Before we have got to the lodge the clouds are rising over Jura, and very rapidly the whole glorious panorama opens upon our view. As the mist disperses the wind freshens, and the sun actually shows signs of vitality after his long sulks. There go eight ravens over our heads, winging their way from the shores of Loch Awe to the distant islands. They may croak away; we have too firm a belief in our luck to be turned from our purpose by their dissonant voices; besides, we are used to them – it seldom happens that a day passes without our seeing or hearing several. They may be trapped upon the mainland; but there are plenty of rocky islands seldom visited where they can breed in peace. I like them better than the jackdaws, which increase and multiply in the same places and for the same reason. The one reminds me of a mastiff; the other of a mischievous yapping cur. I

A woman fishing, by Ernest Briggs

yards off, and, as I had conjectured, the cause of its terror immediately followed in the shape of a splendid hen falcon which swooped close past my head, and, seeing me, soared off with a startled flight, and was soon lost to sight over the neighbouring hill. It was ten minutes and more before the curlew would leave my society, doubtless fearing that its enemy was waiting for it not far off.

But the dog-cart has pulled up at Dunadd Bridge, and it is time that I should get out and put my rod together. As I look at the heavy stream pouring over the rocks above, and through the arches of the bridge, I mentally admit that there is no great hurry about it. My regular marks are covered, and the water is indubitably too high; but it is clear and falling. We can see by the sticks and rubbish left on the bank that it has been higher by three feet during the night, and there is even now hope of a fish in the shallows at the heads and tails of the deep pools; while later, if the day holds up, the water should arrive at a height which will fish well. Why should I despair? My little terrier Punch sets me a lesson of perseverance by dashing off at once after the same rabbit which he always hunts at this place with as much apparent assurance of success as if he had never failed before, and in a minute is digging again at the same old hole into which his enemy has frisked as usual, with a saucy jerk of his tail, as if he enjoyed the joke. Alfred, too, is evidently sanguine, and eager that I should begin, as he has already screwed the landing-net on to the handle; so I sit down, and take out the joints of my rod, a light fourteen-foot greenheart double-handed trout-rod, tie them carefully together, and pass the line through the rings. Next I try each joint of the casting-line, and select the largest Blue Doctor I can find in my book for a tail-fly, and a dropper of attractive appearance, a black dog, rather larger than I usually fish with on this water. The fish here prefer a small fly; but for the present, in this high flood, the great point is to let them have something they can see to attract their attention.

Poor discontented fishermen! We are never satisfied. One day we are sighing for more water, the next we are grumbling because we have too much. 'Depend upon it,' said the present Lord Brampton (then only Mr Hawkins, Q.C.), when acting at the bar for two moneylenders in a scrape, 'your best chance is to tell the truth.'

am tolerant of what keepers call vermin, and would never willingly permit the slaughter of a peregrine or an eagle, although I know they take toll both in moor and forest; but jackdaws and rats are my abhorrence, and any method of destroying them has my hearty acquiescence and good-will. The eagles, alas! seldom if ever pay us a visit; but the peregrine is often with us. Only three days ago, as I was fishing the Irishman's pool, higher up the river, I was startled by the cry of a curlew evidently in distress; and immediately afterwards the bird itself settled on the stones not ten

The day's catch by John Russell

'That's what I tell my son,' answered the eldest of them; 'but I'm afraid he will tell too much truth.' Water, like truth, is an excellent thing in moderation; but whatever may be said of the latter, you may certainly have too much of the former. The provoking thing, too, is that you may have too much one day and not enough on the next. A short Highland river, not running out of a loch, with every hill around it drained with deep sheep-drains, rises and falls almost as fast as a speculative Stock Exchange security. However, there is nothing for it but to begin, and I deposit my spare joints

and my bag almost opposite a rock just showing through the breaking water, and begin to fish the lowest of the three stretches which make up the long pool of Dunadd.

This is a monotonous pool to fish; but too prolific to be neglected. It is rather difficult to manage with a small rod, because the stream is for the most part sluggish, and requires a strong wind to make it properly fishable, which, when it touches the water properly, always blows up stream. Therefore, to make the fly hang right, it is not sufficient to cast straight across. You should throw a long line across and down stream, and work the fly with the point of the rod close to the water; and this must be done often, as the line in such a position will not work long at a time. It is tiresome and monotonous at the best of times, because one part of it is so like another; but today, when it is too high, it is doubly tedious, because I have not that faith in the result which encourages me to persevere, and I only flog on mechanically, in order to give plenty of time for the higher pools to run down. This occupies an hour and a half, during which time nothing makes an offer at the fly except a small parr, which endeavours to hang itself on a hook nearly as big as itself; so it is with a sigh of relief that I shoulder my bag, and with my young companion make my way through a small swampy hazel wood to the next pool up the river, which is known as 'Boy's' pool, in allusion, I believe, to some legendary boy, who is supposed to have met his death there.

This is a pool which, although it always holds fish, is not usually very productive. The stream runs strong at the neck, but the pool immediately after broadens into a round hole, very deep for the most part, out of which two streams run round a sort of gravelly island. This double exit causes a kind of eddy and backwater, and except at the very neck, it is impossible to keep the line straight and make the fly hang naturally. However, I again deposit my baggage, and at the second cast a heavy boil breaks the surface of the water, the line tightens and the reel whirs. Hurrah! I am into my first fish.

I shout to Alfred, who is slowly making his way up the bank, slightly bored at the proceedings so far; and the whole scene changes in an instant. Up he runs, with excitement and delight depicted on his face, just as the salmon makes a furious rush up stream, and then a jump which nearly lands him on the opposite bank. Then comes a lull while the fish sulks for a minute in the deep water in the centre of the pool, and I can assure my little attendant, who is nervously and excitedly screwing the landing-net off and the gaff on, that he has plenty of time. He has been out with me before; but it was only yesterday that he was first allowed to use the gaff, and very well he did it, landing a seven-pound fish at the first attempt. Off goes the salmon again, and after another two turns of the reel, shows himself on the surface – a good fish for this water. I generally minimise the size of my fish, but I calculate his weight at between eight and nine pounds. As he

shows, Alfred dashes to the side and madly dances after him in his rushes, heedless of my shouts that, if he will keep quiet, I will bring the salmon up to him; but it is not to be this time. The fish dashes out of the pool into the stream below, and, without the least preliminary warning, the rod straightens. The hold has given way! A breathless gasp from each of us, and the tears almost rise into my small boy's eyes; but when he sees the disgust expressed upon my countenance – which, in self-defence, I must assert to be more for his sake than my own – he remembers his first duty as consoler, and, fumbling in his pocket for some propitiatory offering, says, 'Never mind, father; take a nut.'

The consolation has come, although perhaps it is not the half-ripe nut that has done it; and, hoping for better luck next time, we move on to the Stance pool, where the stream sweeps round a bend of the river near the road, ending in a wide stretch, with deep water under the opposite bank. Half-way down a small sea-trout takes the dropper and speedily finds his way into the landing-net; and just a few yards before the end, there is another swirl in the water, and the line is tight and the reel again in motion. But it is only for a few seconds. There is something in the feel of the 'hold' that tells me instinctively that the fish is but lightly hooked, and I shake my head at the little gillie, who is already beginning to prepare for action, just before the line comes back slack once more – to my disappointment, but not this time to my surprise. It is rather annoying to have had two fish on and lost them both; but I am not disheartened, as the water is improving every minute, and every one that has risen has taken hold after a fashion. We shall doubtless do better presently.

A walk of a couple of hundred yards brings us to an anonymous pool at the next bend, which is quite as well worthy of attention as many that have high-sounding names. This is a river in which it will not do to rely on tradition and reputation. The banks are undermined and fall in, and tons of gravel are washed down by every spate, so that what is a deep pool one year may become a mere run or shallow the next; therefore, only those places that have some permanent natural features, such as a bridge or a rock, or those that have been the scene of some accident or event, acquire and retain the honour of a name. I can remember catching fish in this pool twenty years ago, and then until last year it was hardly worth fishing; but the opposite side was faced with stone in 1888 to prevent further damage to the bank and the adjoining fields, and it has since become a very good place for fish, with a stream at the top ending in a deep round pool at the bottom. There is an iron railing and a ditch to get over to take me to the gravelly bank at the top, and, as it is lunch-time, I choose a sheltered spot under the bank at the bottom, where I leave my boy to unpack and begin his meal, while I go up and fish the stream over for the first time; but he has not got beyond the stage of taking out the paper parcels and untying the strings when there is another whir of the reel, and a nice little fish is dashing down stream attached (firmly, I hope, this time) to the tail-fly, which bears the seductive name of 'the Captain'. Cake, egg-sandwiches, and cold grouse are flung down at the first sound of the reel, and Alfred comes tearing up with Punch at his heels. The fish runs well, and is soon sufficiently exhausted to bring up to the gaff; but this time the landing is the most serious matter of difficulty. I have said that my boy gaffed his first salmon yesterday, and did it well; but then he had not been worked into a state of excitement by seeing two fish lost. His first attempt is too slow, and with the second he gaffs the casting-line, when if the fish had not been thoroughly exhausted, he would have bidden us farewell; but there is luck in odd numbers, and at the third try the point goes home, and a nice little grilse is deposited on the stones. He is soon weighed and put into the bag. He is only five pounds; but a fish is a fish, and we need no longer fear going home with 'a blank day'.

Lunch is soon over, and, when two more flies have been tried on the same stream without another offer, we begin to retrace our steps down stream. Something, either a large trout or a small 'fish', moved at the fly, just below the place where we had luncheon, and again after a rest and a change of fly; but, whatever he was, he did not mean business, and equally resisted the attractions of a claret-body, a small Jock Scott, and a Captain. However, I got two small trout before I am back to the Stance pool, and give them but a short shrift, as it will be about as much as I can do to finish my water by the time the dog-cart is ordered to meet us at the bridge.

Here fortune is again favourable, for a very pretty fish of a little

over six pounds takes the fly under water in the deepest part, plays kindly, and comes to the gaff soon. The only difficulty this time is caused by the ill-directed zeal of my terrier Punch, who appears to have given up rabbit-hunting for the moment, and, erroneously thinking that he can help me, dashes at the fish every time I bring him near the gaff, sending him flying to the other side of the pool, and sadly disconcerting my attendant, who, however, does his duty nobly, and in spite of the disturbing element, has the salmon out on the bank the first time he gets a fair chance, and deposits him in the bag beside his predecessor, looking like a bar of silver – so bright that he cannot have left the sea many hours.

Another fish, about the same size, rises, and falls to rise no more, in the very next stream, just where the bank has been made up with some piles, and then the luck changes again. The height of the water is still improving, the breeze keeps up well, and the sky is all a fisherman could desire; but – the fish have left off rising. I change my flies half-a-dozen times, trying varieties of size and colour; but neither the Boy's pool nor the stream below, nor any part of the long pool by Dunadd, produces a single rise; and when I see the dog-cart turning the corner towards the bridge, I feel no inclination to keep the rod on the lower water waiting, but take it down at once; and soon we are 'all on board', and I am lighting a meditative pipe, my little boy volubly recounting to the groom the adventures of the day, while Punch, curled up upon the bag under the seat, dreams of the rabbits he could not catch, and of the well-earned meal which awaits him on his return.

So ends an enjoyable day; and if the more fortunate captors of monsters in Canada, Norway, the Tay, the Tweed, laugh at my poor little spoils, I can at least remind them that I am able to use the lightest of tackle, and can do without boat, gillie, and many of the other accessories indispensable on their grand rivers. I have myself been among the twenty-pounders, and can conscientiously say that with treble gut and an eighteen-foot rod I have found them just as easy to catch as their smaller relations in the Add.

A.E. Gathorne-Hardy, *Autumns in Argyleshire*
with Rod and Gun, 1900

Incredible Bigness

The Salmon is ever bred in the fresh Rivers (and in most Rivers about the month of August) and never grows big but in the Sea; and there to an incredible bigness in a very short time; to which place they covet to swim, by the instinct of nature, about a set time: but if they be stopp'd by Mills, Floud-gates or Weirs, or be by accident lost in the fresh water, when the others go (which is usually by flocks or sholes) then they thrive not.

And the old Salmon, both the Melter and Spawner, strive also to get into the Sea before Winter; but being stopt that course, or lost; grow sick in fresh waters, and by degrees unseasonable, and kipper, that is, to have a bony gristle, to grow (not unlike a Hauk's beak) on one of his chaps, which hinders him from feeding, and then he pines and dies.

But if he gets to Sea, then that gristle wears away, or is cast off (as the Eagle is said to cast his bill) and he recovers his strength, and comes next Summer to the same River, (if it be possible) to enjoy the former pleasures that there possess him; for (as one has wittily observed) he has (like some persons of Honour and Riches, which have both their Winter and Summer houses) the fresh Rivers for Summer, and the salt water for winter to spend his life in; which is not (as Sir Francis Bacon hath observed – In his *History of Life and Death*) above ten years: And it is to be observed, that though they grow big in the Sea, yet they grow not fat but in fresh Rivers; and it is observed, that the farther they get from the Sea, the better

they be. And it is observed, that, to the end they may get far from the Sea, either to Spawne or to possess the pleasure that they then and there find, they will force themselves over the tops of Weirs, or Hedges, or stops in the water, by taking their tails into their mouthes, and leaping over those places, even to a height beyond common belief: and sometimes by forcing themselves against the streame through Sluces and Floud-gates, beyond common credit. And 'tis observed by Gesner, that there is none bigger then in England, nor none better then in Thames.

And for the Salmon's sudden growth, it has been observed by tying a Ribon in the tail of some number of the young Salmons, which have been taken in Weires, as they swimm'd towards the salt water, and then by taking a part of them again with the same mark, at the same place, at their returne from the Sea, which is usually about six months after; and the like experiment hath been tried upon young Swallows, who have after six months absence, been observed to return to the same chimney, there to make their

A hooked salmon, by Henry Alken

nests, and their habitations for the Summer following; which hath inclined many to think, that every Salmon usually returns to the same River in which it was bred, as young Pigeons taken out of the same Dove-cote, have also been observed to do.

And you are yet to observe further, that the He Salmon is usually bigger then the Spawner, and that he is more kipper, and less able to endure a winter in the fresh water, then the She is; yet she is at that time of looking less kipper and better, as watry and as bad meat.

And yet you are to observe, that as there is no general rule without an exception, so there is some few Rivers in this Nation that have Trouts and Salmon in season in winter. But for the observations of that and many other things, I must in manners omit, because they will prove too large for our narrow compass of time, and therefore I shall next fall upon my direction how to fish for the Salmon.

And for that, first, you shall observe, that usually he staies not long in a place (as Trouts will) but (as I said) covets still to go

Salmon fishing, by Norman Wilkinson

neerer the Spring head; and that he does not (as the Trout and many other fish) lie neer the water side or bank, or roots of trees, but swims usually in the middle, and neer the ground; and that there you are to fish for him; and that he is to be caught as the Trout is, with a Worm, a Minnow, (which some call a Penke) or with a Fly.

And you are to observe, that he is very, very seldom observed to bite at a Minnow (yet sometime he will) and not oft at a fly, but more usually at a Worm, and then most usually at a Lob or Garden worm, which should be wel scowred, that is to say, seven or eight dayes in Moss before you fish with them; and if you double your time of eight into sixteen, or more, into twenty or more days, it is still the better, for the worms will stil be clearer, tougher, and more lively, and continue so longer upon your hook.

Izaak Walton, *The Compleat Angler*, 1653

Norwegian Giants

It was Sunday evening. As the end of the week drew near we had been anxious as to local customs with regard to fishing on a Sunday – these varying in different parts of Norway. Erik had told us we might fish after dinner; and Gjertrud, our laughter-loving handmaiden who happily seemed to find something comical in almost everything we said and did, propounded the brilliant idea. 'Yes, but you can dine at ten and begin fishing at eleven o'clock.' There was subtlety about this capable of infinite development, but it struck us as too refined, so we delayed starting until four in the afternoon; the greater population of the village, we observed, accompanying us.

When I commenced to cast Stein Pool from the platform, there was an audience of thirty-four folks, lads and lassies, old men and maidens, assembled on the bank behind.

Stein Pool is dead and deep, with a moderate stream running in beyond mid-river, and the fish lying well in towards the opposite bank, which was heavily wooded down to the brink. The nearer half of the river is (in fine water) a deep black set where the line, if allowed to enter, is instantly drowned. This combination necessitates not only long casting, but rapid long throws and quick returns, which means hard work, especially as a high bank, twenty yards behind, involved lifting the line well up in the air. The swish of the line in the faces of the spectators soon cleared them off to safer distances, and about half-way down the pool there came that tug – no, it is not a tug, but a sudden inflexible resistance as of a tree trunk or solid rock. But I knew that a big fish had annexed the fly, deep under and without showing, and delayed not to drive the small double hook well home into his jaws.

Five minutes later, after a prolonged period of bottom fighting, jagging and sulking, alternated with sub-aquatic gymnastics and contortions that kept me trembling for my tackle the captive came

Fishing in Norway, by John Singer Sargent

up with a sudden rush to the surface, ploughing along on his bent broadside for twenty yards. Then we saw that this fish was even bigger than the lost monster of Samkomme. Was it possible to subdue such a salmon on that paltry hook? True, it was double, that reflection seemed inspiring. But then the hooks were smaller than that which had already failed, being actually the smallest (No. 5) in all my collection and therefore specially selected for fine water in a streamless pool.

I determined rightly or wrongly to play for safety, to act solely on the defensive, and to leave the fish to kill himself, even though it involved my spending the night with him in the process.

I pass over details which would involve repetition. Suffice it that the fish, persistently dropping downstream, obliged me to follow. This for some distance was easy enough, but lower down trees grew to the water's edge. Still it was necessary to follow, having some fifty yards of line out. The fish was now in the shallows, rolling heavily at intervals with short, sullen rushes during one of which I felt a slight 'draw' – perhaps the hold of one hook had failed.

W. going down through the trees to reconnoitre reported the fish tired. For almost minutes at a time he lay inert in midstream, suffering himself to be towed ahead in the slack pool-tail without resistance. Had it now been possible to incline the rod inland an opportunity to gaff might, it seemed probable, be secured. But the thickset branches projecting far across the stream forbade this and two alternatives remained. One was to drop still lower downstream trusting to find shallows and get in the cleek at the foot of the pool.

This, however, I rejected, first, because the fish was yet in no sense under control and the danger in the stronger stream obvious, nor was there any reasonable certainty of gaffing there. Secondly, because I knew nothing of the depth or nature of the water below, beyond seeing that there was a strong rapid at least two hundred yards long with an island in midstream and thick wood on either bank. Hence I elected the other course, and endeavoured slowly

to tow the half-beaten fish upstream and thus clear the trees. A stone thrown in below the fish's tail at this point might have served the purpose, but we did not think of it at the time.

While thus engaged, though exerting no special pressure – indeed, humouring the captive in all his little runs and lunges – the rod flew up and the fly came home unharmed. The fight was over and the fish the victor.

A few days after in the Stein Pool, I hooked another monster. I felt him come, struck at the right moment, yet in rather less than a minute, for some reason unexplained, the hook came away. During his short captivity he had made one long surface run thus showing up his size.

The conclusions we came to were these. That these very heavy fish given the best of holds on single gut may take an hour to land and possibly more, and that during so prolonged a pressure the hold of a small hook (in fine water no other is of any use) must almost necessarily wear itself out.

I give for what it may be worth, the quality and rank of the two above named fish, these points being set down by estimate by the local experts. The Samkomme fish, forty pounds, fresh from sea the night before. The Stein Pool fish, a larger salmon, probably from forty to fifty, but of some fourteen days sojourn in the river.

These estimates I take to be fairly near the mark. After landing heavy fish one comes to know the strength and style of the twenty-pounder and of fish ranging between that and thirty pounds.

There are old hands among anglers who never fail to land a fish. They may smile at this record of disaster, pointing out things done that should have been avoided, or neglected that should have been tried. Well, to criticise is easy; so, too, is it to haul out heavy but ill-conditioned autumn fish from the depths of some sluggish hole. But with fresh-run springers in Scandinavian streams the case is different and the difficulty greater and more varied.

Abel Chapman, *Wild Norway*, 1897

Sabie's River

It was a day of wild winds from the northwest, and fishing had been spasmodic. The strong current headed my frail canoe downstream while the gusty air buffetted it from side to side and, as we swung first this way and then that, casting was difficult and uncertain.

After luncheon we headed for a pool below the camp, with the contending elements fighting for the mastery of the light craft. A furry body outlined against the first green of a shorn field attracted our eyes, and we crossed the stream to land for a nearer investigation. Creeping up step by step on the little animal, it was soon revealed to be a groundhog, that fabled prophet of the spring who, with bright, wary eyes, watched us approach until we were distant from him by a scant ten feet, then, without a preliminary show of fear, whisked into the safety of his hole.

The ground was soft and spongy under our returning feet and the river, darkly ruffled by the wind, hurried by impatient to reach the sea. Rather than cross its fast-running surface and fish on the farther side, it was decided to try a cast or two into the deep pool at our feet. The line hissed long and snake-like through the air; then again, and the fly began its slow, jerky, return journey. Suddenly there was a sense of weight, although there had been neither warning swirl nor savage rush to indicate a strike. Yet something alive was surely there, shaking its head in the secret depths. I started to reel in, the fish obeying the pressure with such docility that Alf opined it was another grilse but, from a certain heaviness, I guessed

a small salmon. The canoe grated on the pebbly beach and I stepped ashore, with the unseen captive so near at hand that the landing net was held in readiness. Then a curious thing occurred. Without any telltale sudden rush or startled leap through the air, the line began to move out slowly, steadily, and as irresistibly as if there were no well-built reel checking it nor anxious thumb braking its speed. An invisible force brooked no coercion. First went the enamelled and tapered yards, then the black backing, foot by foot, and nothing I could do served to retard the steady progress. The canoe was held off the shore ready for a hurried departure but, just before it became necessary to use this means of saving my tackle, the long march to the sea came to a temporary end.

There followed thirty-five minutes of a battle that was never sensational, with no jumps clear of the water and no brilliant runs, but a battle in which the fish seemed never to lose his advantage of strength. During that entire time I did not once see my casting line, and even the backing was so far out that the reel-spool was all but bare. The few feet which I gained with greatest effort were lost at once when the next rush came, and for a long time I abandoned all thought of saving the fish and merely hoped for a minimum loss of equipment. Only twice did I see my opponent when there was vouchsafed me a momentary glimpse of a shining black back and a powerful, lashing tail. Then at last the swift current began to show its tiring effect, the pressure became less strong and the runs shorter. When my leader finally showed above the surface of the water, I swung my rod sharply towards the shore where Alf waited with submerged net. Quickly he lifted it and, for a moment, a great body lay across the hoop, then doubled up safe within the strong meshes – twenty-two and one-half pounds of fighting strength vanquished by an eight ounce rod, a light leader, and a line tested to a dead weight of only twelve pounds. And, such is the contrary nature of womankind, when I saw that magnificent, inert creature, I was sorry that I had won, not he, and that he was too tired by the struggle to be put back into his native element once more.

It is curious how an event always attracts an audience, regardless of the location. We are all familiar with the phenomenon of the multitudes which collect about an accident in a sparsely settled countryside, but even that is more comprehensible than the fact of my having had an unexpected witness to this piscatorial battle. The Gains River country is so devoid of humanity that it may well rank as uninhabited; the few who live there are the aged children of hardy pioneers who came, armed with strength and great courage, to wrest a living from the virgin forest soil. Most of the second generation left the bleak land where winter reigns so long for the easier conditions of town life, but here and there one lingers to till the ancestral farms and to keep the trees from encroaching upon the tiny fields, hewn with such labor from the woods. Of these is old Pete Porter, my unexpected spectator, a bachelor of uncounted years who has lived since infancy beside the river. He lives alone there now, in the weather-worn house of his fathers, eking out a precarious livelihood with the scanty produce of the farm – one year like the next, with only the seasons to mark their passing.

Dorothy Noyes Arms, *Fishing Memories,* 1938

Fishing a highland stream, anonymous

The Most Stately Fish

For by cause that the salmon is the most stately fish that any man may angle to in freshwater, therefore I purpose to begin at him.

The salmon is a gentle fish but he is cumbrous for to take. For commonly he is best in deep places of great rivers. And for the most part he holdeth the middle of it that a man may not come at him.

Ye may take him, but it is seldom seen, with a fly, at such time as when he leapeth in like form and manner as ye do take a trout or a graylynge.

Dame Juliana Berners,
A Treatyse of Fysshynge Wyth an Angle, 1496

He's on! Salmon fishing, by Ernest Briggs

Not in a Taking Mood

At times when fish are running up fresh from the sea it is wonderful what freaks they are up to; throwing themselves upwards or sideways, turning somersaults, making tremendous rushes and yet not sporting a bit.

One evening on the Lochy I was returning from the upper part of Number 6 beat to have one more cast over the Sloggan when just above the Fox Hunter's Cottage the river became suddenly alive with fish running about in all directions. I waded in and cast over hundreds; not a fish would come at the fly, but they would, in their jumps, hit the line often enough. After a change or two of flies I gave it up and went on my way to the Sloggan. The first cast there with the same fly I had endeavoured to entice the running fish with, I hooked and landed a bright, fresh run salmon of 10 lb.

Edward Hamilton, *Recollections of Fly Fishing,* 1884

Leaping Salmon, by Robin Armstrong

Tweed Fifty Pounder

In the month of July, some thirty years ago, one Duncan Grant, a shoemaker by profession, who was more addicted to fishing than to his craft, went up the way from the village of Aberlour, in the north, to take a cast in some of the pools above Elchies Water. He had no great choice of tackle, as may be conceived; nothing, in fact, but what was useful, and scant supply of that. Duncan tried one or two pools without success, till he arrived at a very deep and rapid stream, facetiously termed 'the Mountebank': here he paused, as if meditating whether he should throw his line or not. 'She is very big', said he to himself, 'but I'll try her; if I grip him he'll be worth the hauding'.

He then fished it, a step and a throw, about halfway down, when a heavy splash proclaimed that he had raised him, though he missed the fly. Going back a few paces, he came over him again, and hooked him. The first tug verified to Duncan his prognostication, that if he was there 'he would be worth the handing'; but his tackle had thirty plies of hair next the fly, and he held fast, nothing daunted. Give and take went on with dubious advantage, the fish occasionally sulking.

The thing at length became serious; and, after a succession of the same tactics, Duncan found himself at the Boat of Aberlour, seven hours after he had hooked his fish, the said fish fast under a stone, and himself completely tired. He had some thoughts of breaking his tackle and giving the thing up; but he finally hit upon an expedient to rest himself, and at the same time to guard against the surprise and consequence of a sudden movement of the fish.

He laid himself down comfortably on the bank, the butt end of his rod in front; and most ingeniously drew out part of his line, which he held in his teeth. 'If he tugs when I'm sleeping', said he, 'I think I'll find him noo'; and no doubt it is probable he would. Accordingly, after a comfortable nap of three or four hours,

Young fisherman, by John Singer Sargent

Gentlemen fishing, by Henry Alken

Duncan was awoken by a most unceremonious tug at his jaws. In a moment he was on his feet, his rod well up, and the fish swattering down the stream. He followed as best he could, and was beginning to think of the rock at Craigellachie, when he found to his great relief that he could 'get a pull on him'. He had now comparatively easy work; and exactly twelve hours after hooking him, he cleiked him at the head of Lord Fife's water: he weighed fifty-four pounds, Dutch, and had the tide lice upon him.

William Scrope,
Days and Nights of Salmon Fishing in the Tweed, 1843

Perfect Days

First Fish

Recently, at dinner, a friend asked me just when I caught my first fish with a fly. It was a while before I could answer, because the thought put me into reverie and I caught that first trout again before I came back to earth and told him. I suppose the thing began when I had my first day-dreams.

The pine tree seemed very tall then and the song of the yellow-hammer from the top of the thorn had a music in it that made tears come to my eyes for no reason at all except, perhaps, that it was sad, and I was sometimes a melancholy child. Along the lower side of the stackyard field there ran a burn or stream. The burn was a magic place, for here the pied wagtail nested on the bank below the old hawthorns and, rafted on a submerged branch, there was the waterhen's nest. Voles tunnelled the bank and once in a while the otter came sliding up the stream to prowl after trout that might have journeyed so far to spawn. Eels there were in this burn – the ditcher shovelled them out when he cleaned the waterway – but the eels, I think, were never caught by the otter, for I doubt whether the otter's taste is quite so plebeian.

The burn was fed, along its course, by drains that spouted cold clear water from the black earth of the hill-side. Below one of these feeding drains there was always a depression in the bed of the burn where waterweeds trailed. I came upon one of these while looking for the nests of birds and discovered my first trout feeding on insects. I remember that afternoon. The rooks were on the turnip hills pulling the young plants newly thinned and hoed. I watched that little fish for a long time. The world stood still, the sound of the water put everything else out of my mind. I no longer heard the far-off lowing of the cattle, the barking dog, the creaking and jolting of the cart on the road.

When I went home, at last, I thought about that fish. I had time enough to think and dream, for I was barely old enough for school, but old enough to be restless when my elders had their afternoon nap; old enough to love scones and heather honey; old enough to find the settle hard and uncomfortable as a church pew. It was on the settle that I found the hook, a little fishing hook fallen from the coat or hat of some fishing enthusiast who had sat there listening to my grandfather's stories of long ago. It was the sort of hook commonly used at that time. It was fastened to gut. It had once been a respectable fishing fly but the dressing had fallen in ruins. It was all but a bare hook. I put it in a matchbox for further examination and went back the next day to watch that fish again where he had moored himself to intercept any fly or insect that sailed over him. I began to feed my fish with woodlice, beetles, anything, in fact, that would make him break the surface or dash to gulp it down. He was like myself, I suppose, an innocent creature with all the world to learn. He was eager and greedy, but already stunted, I fancy, like most of the trout in little waters. After I had thought for a while I found a piece of white thread and tied the thread to the gut in order to

Fishing the weir, by Frank Teller

Leaping trout, by Frank Teller

lower my first offering to the trout. I had no rod. The fly I impaled and sought to drift to him was a yellow-brown fly that trout anglers call the Cow-dung fly. I hardly need say where it is to be caught. It wasn't easy to sail the fly to the trout, and for some reason, even when I managed to achieve this object, the little fish didn't jump at it with the wild delight he displayed when other flies came sailing down.

It took perhaps a dozen journeys before the fish sprang at the fly and then there he was, alive and leaping, vibrating the taut thread I held in my hand, skipping and dancing out of the water and making me so excited that I slipped and fell into the burn above his hole, but I was used to getting wet in drains and ditches, used to the cold water of the well wetting the arms of my coat and trickling down my chest. I scrambled up and tugged my fish to the bank. I had caught him, and he, little yellow and red-marked trout, had caught me, once and for all. I studied him, laid him on a leaf of fern, moistened his skin again when the magic hue of his wet freshness faded. Life was wonderful indeed. I had caught a fish by watching how a fish feeds, and not the way I had seen other people catch them, with a midden worm or with a wire, or simply by tickling him in his bolt below the bank, even if this art, too, required some skill.

Ian Niall, *Trout from the Hills,* 1961

Paradise

Among the mountains in the south of the South Island of New Zealand lies Lake Te Anau – a narrow lake thirty miles long, of great depth, a cold lake; it is fed by numerous snow rivers, southernmost of all the Clinton River.

The water of the Clinton River is crystal clear; the bottom of its deepest pools, 30 to 40 ft deep, is not obscured, only blued by it: high above, 4000 to 5000 ft on either side, can be seen its source, ice and snow. Its bed is of clean white gravel and sand, except where dark green moss covers the stones. Its banks are covered with a thick forest and undergrowth of tree ferns and many other kinds, very damp, very beautiful, very luxuriant, almost impenetrable. The river is 6 yd wide, on an average 10 ft deep, but long shallows are by no means rare, as are also deep pools; the current is swift. Great forest trees everywhere overhang the water, and dying, fall into the river, to stretch out gaunt arms under water, or, carried by some flood, lie stranded on the shallows, dark brown against the white bed. Great brown trout live in the lake. These ascend the river to spawn, and finding pleasant quarters here sheltering under the submerged trees, feeding on the insects which drop from the foliage above and on the quantities of ephemerides which live amongst the stones and moss of the river-bed, these fish, instead of returning to the lake, settle down to spend the summer in the river. They have been wooed with many kinds of flies and baits, but only by the net have they been brought to bank. Nevertheless, it is impossible to persuade the angler not to fish if he has once seen these grand fish in the crystal water.

On 1 February I forced my way through the bush, and, choosing a place where the water was not too deep, entered the river. Wading cautiously upstream, I soon spotted a fish lying close under my bank beside a sunken tree. I cast many flies over his nose, both wet and dry, large and small; he was asleep. At last I awoke him; he sailed slowly to the other side of the river. Wading up I, in like manner, disturbed two more. Number 3 calmly gazed on an imitation beetle for a little while: that was all. It was now about eleven o'clock; I was seated on a boulder, sadly thinking – thinking about these fish. Did they ever feed? If so, when, and on what?

It was then that I first saw a dun on the water; quickly others appeared, and very soon I saw a great neb break the surface on the far side of the water – my questions were soon answered. The dun was three-quarters of an inch across the wings; body, a very dark olive, almost black; wings, very long, and of an even dark smoky colour; three sets; a brother of our blue-winged olive, so I called him the black-winged black. At once I got out my fly tying book and soon had three fair imitations made. (A waterside fly-tying outfit is valuable at home, but in a strange country an absolute necessity.) Entering the water, I soon found a rising fish above me. Placing the fly in front of him he at once took it; deliberately tightening on him, I got a firm hold; he ran 10 yd, no more, upstream, disappeared under a log by the riverside, and was seen no more. A new fly placed over a new fish resulted similarly, except that the tree was in mid-stream, and opposite to me. I was fishing with the finest undrawn gut, a Mayfly cast; however, salmon gut would not have saved them. I now decided to choose a less snaggy part of the river, mid-stream. I could feel the fish round the corner, but the water was too deep to wade out, so I couldn't clear the line. Very soon I felt that sickening slackness in the rod top – another fly gone. Having now lost all the flies I had tied, I had to sit down and tie some more. However, I saved some time by eating my lunch at the same time.

Passing further upstream – it is far easier written than done, for it means fighting through the bush in those places where wading is impossible, a frequent occurrence – I came to a great pool, very deep, and bordered on my side by a cliff. At the head I saw a great fish, 12 lb at least, rising, taking duns, a wonderful sight. How gracefully he moved his great bulk from side to side and up and down! In order to cast to him I had to get down the cliff, and whilst doing so I loosened a good piece of ground, which came tumbling down with me, splash into the water, fortunately shallow at this spot – the fish was gone.

A little above this pool's head, at the tail of the pool above and in front, of a submerged tree, I found a good fish rising. To get within casting distance I found it necessary to walk out into the water on the tree, for all around it was too deep for wading. Standing thus, I put the fly over the fish. Slowly and unsuspectingly he sucked it in. I was afraid he would take cover under my feet, so when I tightened on him I at the same time stood up and waved my free arm. This had the desired effect; he fled upstream, where I knew all was clear, so I let him go. At about 50 yd he stopped, and I began to pull him down. It

Brown trout, by Richard Smith

now became apparent that I could not land him where I was, standing on a snag. I must get up to the fish. There was only one way – by stepping down from my perch. It is very hard to judge the depth of clear water. I stepped. Down I went to half-way up my chest. I struggled upstream, holding the little 8 ft rod high in the air. I was pleased to find the water getting shallower, and the fish still on, and after several heavy rushes and a couple of jumps, or rather plunges, I had him beat, all except for the final tiring out, which took a minute or two, and then he was mine – 6 lb.

Chilled by the icy water, having caught as many fish as I could drag through the bush (four fish weighing 18 lb), the hatch of fly now beginning to lessen, a thirst for some hot tea overtaking me, having drained my waders by sitting down with my feet cocked up against a tree, I decided to collect the dead and make for home, and thus finish a perfect day's dry-fly fishing.

The next day, between 11 and 12 p.m., I had two fish, 6 lb and 8 lb, and one break by a fish of about 4 lb – the latter fish was bulging, and would not take a dry fly. Instead of troubling to tie a nymph, I cut down a small March Brown I had in my fly box; quite a good nymph can be made in this way – cut the wings down until only the stumps remain, cut off all the hackle as short as possible, reduce the whisks by two-thirds. The third or fourth time over the fish followed down and took it; as he turned I tightened up – down went the fish past me, making the line whiz on the water, down, down and across. I could see his home now – below me, and on the

The rise, by Winslow Homer

far side a group of sunken trees. I put all the drag on I dared, and managed to hold him a few yards from home. In this way we remained for quite ten seconds, the fish swimming for all he was worth, and at the other end I holding on. At last the fish turned and came towards me; I gathered in some line and was glad of a breather. Suddenly, round went the fish, and, taking me quite by surprise, got home before I could stop him; the line came back minus the fly. I never felt less sorry at losing a fish. Then the rain began, so I made an end.

There are only two flies in this cream of fishing – the bush, which makes a labour of walking and much of the water utterly unapproachable, and the sand flies. These small black flies are busy from sunrise to sunset, their bite is painful, the bump they raise very irritable; they gradually collect round the angler until quite a cloud surrounds him, and he has to beat a hasty retreat into the bush in order to give them the slip.

Thus I found Paradise.

J.C. Mottram, *Fly-Fishing: Some New Arts and Mysteries,* 1921

Back to Basics

For many years I thought fishing small flies was all about casting the right fly. I thought the right fly pattern was a silver bullet that would solve all my problems. Of course, it didn't.

Now I think the answer includes the fly pattern, but also how that pattern is used. I've learned that, with small flies, it often comes down to just matching the size of what the trout are eating and then presenting it in a way that matches, or more accurately doesn't disrupt, their feeding behavior. You must get the fly to where the trout expects it to be and manipulate it in a way that doesn't look unusual to the trout. Needless to say, a perfect match of the natural won't hurt you, but you really do have to get it to where the trout is looking for it. There is a kind of match-the-hatch mythology among small-fly fishers that can be counterproductive if you don't include presentation. Don't fall into the trap.

Fishing small flies should be concise. Don't waste any motion. Include just the necessary elements. Think of it like a drawing. You wouldn't want to see any unnecessary lines, would you? Or consider it as a machine. I'd wonder about a machine that included unnecessary parts. Reduce everything

Taking a fly, by WJS

to the basics. Determine what you need for where you fish, know how to use it, have confidence in it, and leave the rest in the truck. For years I carried a vest full of fly boxes, doodads, and gizmos. After a while I started leaving some of the fly boxes that I thought I wouldn't need in the truck. I reasoned that if I ended up really wanting them I could just walk back to the parking area, which was never that far away, and get them. Over time I found myself leaving more and more stuff in the truck. And I have never returned to get any of it.

Reducing the stuff will give you the freedom to concentrate on the trout, or more precisely, the prey. Small-fly angling at its best is trout stalking and trout hunting. You would do well to think of yourself as a predator. Go light, lay low, get small, follow your instinct, and temper your fly fishing with artistry.

Put as little as you can between the trout and yourself.

Ed Engle, *Fishing Small Flies,*
2005

The Ones That Got Away

A Gallant Fight

This it is that makes salmon fishing so enticing and so exciting. In many salmon rivers there is but little to prevent a fair fisherman killing a big fish, but in some, the Spean in Inverness-shire for instance, the case is very different. Here a big fish has all the advantage. Just get a twenty-five or thirty pounder on your line, and see what will happen; it is twenty to one in favour of the salmon.

I once lost a fish after three hours and forty minutes' hard work, and this is how it happened. Whilst playing a fish of 14 lb in the Coa Pool on the Spean, a huge salmon, bright as silver, jumped over my line, and almost immediately another, its fellow, not quite so big, showed himself a little lower down. After landing the fourteen pounder it was too late, and the pool had been too much disturbed to try for these monsters, but on the morrow, on arriving at the Boat Pool, I noticed a peculiar smile on the fisherman's countenance, and as we crossed, he said, 'I think we will go at once to the Coa, and try for the big one, not that we shall land him if we do hook him, for we never have, and I believe never shall land such as he in this river.'

'Why,' I said, 'what do you think their respective weights were?'

'Well,' he said, 'from forty to fifty pounds.' Well, away we went; he took great pains in putting the rod together, in choosing a good casting line, and in selecting, after a careful examination of his book, a fly from his cap which he said my lord L. had lost a big fish

with, a day or two ago. After a short time I managed the cast – all who know the Coa pool will understand what I mean by 'the cast' – it is a very long and difficult one because your fly must drop close to a certain stone on the further side of the pool. I won't say how many yards you have to get out, because people are apt to exaggerate, but it is a very long cast, and that will suffice, particularly as there is a big bank and bushes close behind. As the fly came round there was an awful swirl, the line tightened, and I felt I had him, or more properly speaking, as is shown in the sequel, he had me. Aitken threw up his arms and shouted, 'I do believe you have got the big one.' There was a run about the pool for a minute or two, and then with a whirl and a swirl away he went, taking out ninety yards of line, and with a tremendous leap, showing us what he was, he stopped short, and came with a rush back again, so that winding up was a difficulty. 'Ah,' said Aitken,

The gillie, from an anonymous painting

'he is not the biggest, but it is the other, and we shall never land him; we must try to keep him up in these pools; if he once goes to the rapids we are done.' For three hours and twenty minutes he led us a pretty dance up and down, never able to get him up into the deep part of the Coa Pool, where we might have had a chance. At last away he went over the rapids, down into Tumbledown, and after a race or two all round that pool, away again as hard as he and we could go into the next, pool. Now if the casting line will only hold, we may still get him, when suddenly the line came away without the hook, the gut fairly rubbed into a shred, and so the fish beat us, and after three hours and forty minutes we had to throw in the sponge – not in shame, for it was a gallant fight; he was not hooked foul, for twice we brought him almost to the surface, and saw the hook was in his jaw; but he, as many a big fish has done before in this river, simply beat us.

Edward Hamilton, *Fly Fishing*, 1884

River fishing, by Norman Wilkinson

Attached to a Submarine

Towards the end of September following my first Tweed adventure of August, I was once more sent up to the Border by my father in charge of the man of Peebles. This time I was armed with huge and formidable rods and vast and gorgeous flies which excited me even to look at them.

In effect, it was intended that I should have the chance of catching a salmon despite the fact that I was quite incapable at that time of handling the honest 18 ft of greenheart (made in the year 1865) with which I was supposed to cast a vast Durham Ranger or a stupendous Wilkinson. I can still remember my exact feelings on that misty September morning so long ago, as I sat in a boat with old Tom who rowed with those short, non-feathering strokes peculiar to those who row rather light boats against fast rough streams towards the 'break in the Cauld', the famous break in the famous Cauld on the Scotch side nearly opposite Pot Point at Twizell which was the cause of Old Tom's lengthy harangue against 'Scotties' and the dyers of Galashiels. A wonderful morning, a small boy holding a vast rod, going to catch a salmon (or so he thought). If I had been St George going out to kill his first dragon I could not have been more excited – or happier. The rod, the reel and the line with which I fished that day are worthy of a few words of remembrance. The rod was 18 ft of greenheart, or possibly greenheart and hickory, and extremely heavy; yet with all its weight it was a delightful rod to cast with (I many times used it in after years) for a full-grown

man if hopelessly outsize for a boy of twelve. It was only necessary with these old rods to hold the thing upright and just flick the point forward and one could cast a sufficiently long line with no effort at all. There is a popular belief that the old rods were very tiring to use: personally I have always found a light rod much more tiring for salmon fishing. But that September morning in 1910 I experienced some difficulty in casting and I do not suppose my fly worked in quite the approved manner. The line I used on that occasion was a unique relic; a simply glorious line of real plaited horsehair of indefinite age and of a noble blackness, oiliness and mellowness; the perfect line for use with a big rod on a big river. The old reel or rather 'winch' that held this line was also a beautiful piece of work if somewhat massive.

The particular cast I fished that morning, the 'break in the Cauld', is one of the easiest places to fish on the Tweed. One fishes it from the land, from the stones of the Cauld itself, and a glorious rush of semi-broken water between the Cauld and the Scotch bank makes the working of one's fly quite automatic. It is one of those places where one is very likely to get into a fish on almost any

Salmon river, by Vincent R. Balfour Brown

suitable spring or autumn day, but for some reason it is not a cast which produces its five or six fish in the day as does Pot Point further down on the Twizell beat.

With a beating heart I fished down the 'break in the Cauld', feeling certain that any moment I should see a huge salmon rise at my fly like a trout and be hooked. I did not realise then that, with the old heavy hair line which I was using, my fly must have been fishing nearer the bottom of the stream than the top. In any case, after half an hour's casting and a change of flies, old Tom decided

that we had better try down below on the Border Maid cast. Getting into the boat, the river soon took us down to this delightful run on the Scotch side rather below Pot Point. As we passed Pot Point old Tom pointed out a jutting stone where once upon a time he said he had hooked four salmon one after the other, each time with his foot on the end of the stone, and landed them all. It was at this point that many years ago old Tom, when netting a fish for one of the syndicate members, actually lifted out a fresh unhooked fish by mistake, while the hooked fish still remained in play. The reason of course was that a fresh fish was following closely behind the fish which was being played. The lucky member therefore had two fish instead of one. I believe that this, while not a common happening, is by no means unknown on the Tweed and other rivers where a large net is used instead of a gaff.

I remember that when I had made about half a dozen casts on Border Maid and just as I had turned to speak to old Tom, I felt that I had hooked a snag. I suddenly realised that the point of the great old rod was bending, and then – then 'Ye have him!...' A shout from old Tom and a swirl in the current, 10 yd away, and I was into my first salmon. It was nothing like what I had expected, so much slower than the rise of a trout and a great impression of heaviness. To a small boy at the bottom of a huge rod that autumn fish did feel heavy. It felt as if I had become attached to a submarine or something. The rod bent and then bent more, and the old 'winch'

began to croak like a raven. Quite slowly but most inevitably the fish cruised away down-stream and across towards the English side. 'Keep your point up; keep it up, keep a hold on him...' Old Tom seemed to me unnaturally calm and unmoved by the momentous thing which was happening to me. 'Just keep a hold of him...' I remember that I felt as if I was near the end of a particularly violent quarter-mile. And for an agonising and glorious ten minutes that leisurely battle went on with old Tom gently keeping the boat and a very dour old autumn fish never showing himself, and moving about in an entirely unexcited manner. And then, most undramatically, my rod-point straightened, the taut black hair line slackened and the fight was over. With a sob I wound in and the groaning of the huge winch sounded to me more awful than any tolling bell. I remember asking old Tom how big he thought the fish had been. 'Maybe thirty pound.' My heart gave one more miserable throb – my cup was full. 'He was maybe hookit in the gib – terrible hard mouths the old kippers have...' Resignedly old Tom turned the boat across the up-stream and rowed me up to a rather sad lunch-time below the overhanging rocks of Pot Point, while old Tom himself 'hirpled' off up the path to his cottage.

The man of Peebles said little but his mien was stern and sad: 'Master George, you'll likely not have hold of a salmon like that again for years...' And the word 'years' from these bearded lips had a lugubrious, infinitely regretful length.

I did not know then how right he was: it was ten years before I again hooked a salmon.

And so at twelve years of age I made the acquaintance of Tweed, Tweedside characters and language, ancient and beautiful hair lines, 'winches' and vast rods, and the whole Border atmosphere, Flodden Field, Tillmouth, 'Scotties' – and above all, a dour autumn salmon that I never saw. Once more in the Minerva I and the man of Peebles went south past the ever-watching Cheviots.

George Brennand, *Halcyon*, 1947

A giant from the River Eden, anonymous photographer

Cannibal

L et me never fish again if a big trout should catch me without a net! Being taken by a fish one simply cannot land is the most mortifying experience an angler can have, whether he is a philosopher or not.

I remember the afternoon this happened to me. I had been weary long before noon and reduced to despair through my line sinking so often that I was ready to give up before the afternoon sun had begun to look over my shoulder, but I went to fish in that corner where I had taken so many fine trout and stood a while watching the odd fish rising far out in the little bay. While I was doing this I saw a fish rise close in under the rocks. It was a good fish. The rise was characteristic of a big fish in that lake. I didn't wait but flicked the line on to the water with a backhand cast. The fly bounced against the rock face and dropped within two or three inches where, a second before, the fish had risen. Before I could balance my body the fish had taken the fly. I let line go, recovered my balance and began to play the fish. It was well hooked and ran first to the left and then to the right, keeping perhaps four or five inches below the surface but making no attempt to go down. It passed me quite close on the third or fourth occasion and I was astonished to see

Salmon on the bank, by Denys Watkins Pitchford

the sort of fish I was into. Here was a fish that some people might have called a cannibal. I began to guess as to its girth and weight. In any other water it could have been a salmon, I felt. Minutes passed and it came quite close to the side. I was able to look down on it and see the almost casual movement of fins, tail and mouth as it gaped.

It is a strange thing that many a well-hooked fish reserves its final strength for the moment when it is about to be captured. Let a fish run. Let it have line and tire it out in taking it. Bring it back under strain, but if it wants to, let it run again, let it run. There is no mystery in the business of playing a fish but one small fear assails me on these occasions. The hook, being a fly hook and not a treble, has time, through the fish moving first to the right and then to the left, through varying strain and the struggles of the fish to free himself, to work a hole and, unless it is burying itself deep in firm jaw, it may come out. One rarely learns why a fish gets away. Essentially it gets away because the hook comes out and the answer is to take no more time in handling a fish than is necessary to bring it, subdued, to the net or gaff.

This time I had no net or gaff. When the trout looked at me, hovering above the water with my rod curved as only a beautiful split cane rod can curve, it decided to be off again and this time it went down, straining the line over its back as it shook its head. A big trout shakes its head like a water spaniel, or a worrying dog, I always feel. It grows to be a big trout by learning how to live. In a minute my monster was free. I hardly saw him go. He moved into the deeps steadily and quite unlike a small trout when he has broken free. He didn't come back and he hasn't come back on any of the occasions I have waited for him in that place. Other trout have risen to the fly. I have caught dozens there since, but the big one has never been there when I was there and fishing for a big trout.

One remembers that big trout are where they are found and have to be offered the fly at that time. They also have to be netted! A small trout can be lifted out. A trout of three-quarters of a pound may be handlined or horsed along to be beached where the shore allows, but a big trout isn't to be played with. Give him enough time to tire him, and try to bring him out by hand, and you will discover that he still has enough kick to break the cast or straighten the hook! Give him anything but respect and he will go back to the place from whence he came, a wiser creature, better able to elude you on the next occasion.

Why do some trout anglers carry no net when they go off to remote lakes? I fear that the whole business depends so much on signs and omens, and the days when one is blessed are so few that it tempts providence to some of their minds to carry a net.

Ian Niall, *Trout from the Hills,* 1961

Fishing in a tempest, by Richard Ansdell

Getting Started

My first introduction to fly-fishing was with the sea trout, and it came about in this way: Forty-two years ago, strolling down Princes Street, Edinburgh, I came to a shop in which the goods were being sold by auction. The lot then selling was 'a beautiful fly rod, reel, book of flies, line, and basket, all going for ten shillings'. I bid six-pence more and the lot was mine, and I became the happy possessor of what to me at that time was a white elephant.

I had never fished. The lot was deposited in a cupboard. I will not say what I thought of myself in cooler moments for having thrown away what was then to me a considerable sum. However, some few weeks after, strolling along the banks of the Eden in Fifeshire, I came upon a fisherman, and after watching him casting his fly and killing some fine sea trout, the thought struck me: Why not try and do the same with the lot in the cupboard; it appears very easy. So that evening the fishing paraphernalia were rummaged out, and the next morning I made an early start for the river. No one there to give me a hint what to do; but the rod was put together, the line run through the rings, the reel adjusted, the casting line clumsily attached, and a fly selected from the book, I well recollect, a green body and grey wings, and I tried to cast the line into the stream.

Well, never shall I forget that first cast. Not having secured the top joint, that and the line shot well into the river. And again I soon found the fly entangled in the line; that was got clear; then when casting again I found no fly at the end of the line! Another was put on: a peculiar kind of crack behind me when casting and lo this fly was gone. What was to be done? Try another fly: no better result. First it hit a stone, then the line got tangled into strange knots that took half-an-hour to unravel; patience was getting exhausted – the whole lot shall go to the first boy I meet – the Art of fly-fishing was too much for me. Another cast, however, to see whether I could not be more successful. To my surprise the fly went out straight into the ripple, there was a break of the water, and the line tightened. Fortunately the Reel was free. Away went the line, the rod bent – I had hooked a fish, and after most gentle and patient working, I landed a beautiful silvery sea trout of a pound and a half. How I managed it I cannot tell, but I drew him gently out to

River with anglers, by William Jones

a flat bit of sand, threw the rod down, and rushed at my prey, and with both hands cast him far away from the water. This gave me courage. With a short line I found I could get the fly on the water, and in about an hour or so had managed to land three fish without losing another fly. I came home in triumph, and prided myself on knowing how to throw a fly, but was soon disabused of this bit of conceit. The next day dire misfortune awaited me: flies were whipped off, the line got twisted, a large fish broke me in the first rush. I was in despair, when, as fortune would have it, I met the fisherman I had seen the first day, entered into conversation with him, and related my mishaps. At once he gave me every encouragement, pointed out faults, made me fish and throw the fly whilst he gave directions, and with the utmost patience gave me some most valuable hints, and from that time I looked upon fly-fishing as a sport not to be despised, and no one could become a more enthusiastic lover of the Rod and Line.

Edward Hamilton, *Fly Fishing*, 1884

Sea Trout

Red-letter Day

We pass over the spider bridge; panning the river below a capital salmon pool, on through the fir clump, and what a view breaks upon us! There lies the loch in all its beauty, its waters dark blue, a steady breeze ruffling its surface, on one side the mountains (they are more than hills) crowned with basaltic precipices, come sheer down to the water's edge; on the other, grand boulders covered with lichen and dwarf birch, a sloping wood on one of the spurs of Ben y Hatton, reaches to the shore, the birches and oaks ascending and ascending till lost in moor and rugged rocks, and far above us, among the clouds, the craggy summit of the Ben himself. We reach the boat, everything in readiness, and we push off, and slowly row to the opposite side.

A nice breeze favours us as we drift across, with just enough movement of the oars to keep the boat in position. Two flies are used, and we go to work. After a cast or two, we are both fast in fish. My companion has hold of the big one; mine is soon in the boat, and on the next cast up comes a whopper, and now comes the fun: a tremendous rush – a grand leap – another and another, and he is off. We part company, but not before I have been able to guess his size, nearer four than three pounds. W. has in the meantime landed, or rather boated, his fish, a nice fresh-run one of 22 lb.

We have drifted too near the shore, so put back, rowing close in, and again drift over the same fishing ground. Sea trout congregate together in shoals, and whilst playing fish you may miss many a feeding fish, so it is well to go over the same beat twice. We again get four good fish, all over a pound, and then away to other water. As we row gently up, about thirty yards from the shore, I get two good trout, and W. raises either a very large one or a grilse – he is on for a few seconds, a furious rush, and he is gone. We notice three or four salmon jumping a little higher up, throw carefully over them, but with no effect (salmon seldom rise

Salmon fishing in the Highlands, by Richard Ansdell

in this loch), and we then row over to the south side to the Rock and First bay. Here sport begins in earnest, and before leaving we have ten fish, not one under a pound, of which three are between two and three pounds, and one just over three pounds. I was fishing with a Black Palmer with red body and gold twist, and a small Harriet; my companion, a Brown Palmer and Green Mantle, green body, grey mallard wings, silver twist; the fish rose fast and furious, and a good many got off. We then drift across to some weeds, and here every cast brought up a fish, all large. Some are killed, others get off, all fight furiously, and we increase our bag by eight good fish. Whilst drifting, I noticed a large fish rise much further out in the deep water, we at once row to the spot. At the first cast up he comes, and he is fast. With a swirl and a whirl, away he goes, taking out line at a rapid rate, but never showing himself till many yards had been run out, – he must be a salmon! Then comes a mighty leap, and I see by the twist of his tail that he is a trout, but a big one. Leap after leap, still further he goes. Row, row, he'll take out all the line! He fights a glorious fight. But he is well hooked, and he is gradually brought alongside, and after another game struggle for his life he is brought on board; six pounds and a fresh-run fish.

The wind has now dropped, and we row ashore to lunch under some big rocks fallen I wonder how many years ago, and where a spring of ice-cold water gushes out. After luncheon, light our pipes, watch the wild goats clambering over the rocks half-way up the mountain, headed by their hoary grey-bearded patriarch, whose horns now adorn my hall – but stop; look! what are those birds? Three cormorants – wending their way up to the island at the head of the loch. Terrible poachers are these birds; so it is decided, more especially as there is but little breeze, to have a cormorant stalk. So putting up one rod, whilst with the other I pretend to be fishing, W. lies down in the bow, and we gradually near the island, and in this way get within forty yards or so, when all three birds slowly rise. Too late for two of them – one falls dead to the first barrel, and another, mortally wounded, flies away, and dies in the wood. We pick up the dead one, the old mother, and

Casting, by Henry Alken

row gently on to the furthest point for the chance of a duck in the reeds. I am landed; creep quietly up to the edge of the rock, whilst W. in the boat rounds the point. The moment the head of the boat clears the rock up get five ducks. I get one, and W. another as he wheels round, forty yards overhead, a splendid shot. In going to pick mine up I flush and bag a snipe, and a little further on we get two flappers out of the reeds. Now the breeze has freshened, the guns are covered up, and we commence fishing. Drifting down the loch, the wind at our backs, fish are still on the rise, and we take some fine fresh fellows. Suddenly, as is often the case, the wind dies quite away, and the lake is as smooth as a mill pond. Not a fish is stirring, where a few minutes before every cast brought up a trout, so we land and weigh our fish. One six pounds, one over three pounds, eight from two to three pounds, and the rest from three-quarters to a pound and a half. As we walk down the river we have a cast in the Big Pool. The salmon are jumping in all directions – but it is no go – so we wind up, jump into the dog-cart, and return home, well satisfied with our day's sport, and well we may be. It is one of the red-letter days in my journal.

As previously stated, one of the best sea trout lochs on the west coast of Scotland is Loch Ailt. When I first fished that loch I tried the usual sized sea trout flies. Not a rise could I get. Old Angus quietly remarked, 'they are too small.' I gave him my book, and he picked out two flies with which I had been killing salmon on the Lochy. I at once began to take fish, and some very large ones, and a splendid day's sport I had, taking twenty-five as fine sea trout as one could wish to see. I have fished this loch for many years, and invariably find that large flies are necessary for sport. The sea trout run very big, as heavy as ten pounds. Fish of five, six, and seven pounds are not uncommon.

In Loch Coolin and Loch Clair, in Ross-shire, large flies take well, but in Loch Margie, six miles further on, much smaller flies are more general. In Loch Morar the sea trout and salmon in the autumn rarely take the fly, but with the Blue Phantom Minnow you may get good sport. In lochs the sea trout congregate near the weeds, and sport is always the best when fishing near them. In rivers they like the eddies formed by a rapid stream, and the tails of the pools.

Edward Hamilton, *Fly Fishing*, 1884

In the Western Isles

If there are fairly deep pools and long stretches of deep still water, the fish collect in them when the water is low, and if there is a breeze, which blows fairly up or down the stream and so makes a good ripple, a very good basket may be made.

Even when there is no breeze and a bright sun, it is possible to have some sport with the small class of sea trout known as 'herling' and by various other names. These smaller fish run later than most of the large ones, and are often met with in shoals. They average only between half a pound and three-quarters of a pound, but they fight with extraordinary activity and strength, and they sometimes rise when no other fish thinks of doing so. I was once by a small sea trout river on one very hot bright day in August. The streams were shrunken and weak, the still places were smooth as glass, and the water, as is the case in bare rocky parts of the Western Islands, was very little tinged with peat and exceptionally clear. The fish were in the river, but there was only depth enough for them in quite still water, and to fish in that seemed hopeless. I sat down and opened my box of flies.

Ordinary sea trout flies seemed double their proper size on such a day and by such water. One could not think of trying them, and one shuddered at the thickness of undrawn gut, and yet there was the river, and the day, and the fish, and I was alone and seven miles from the lodge. Something had to be done. So I took out a well-tapered trout cast ending in fine drawn gut, and added about a yard of transparent stout gut to the thick end of it. On the fine end I put a plain black hackle fly of a size suitable for brown trout. A really heavy basket was of course out of the question, and I did not rise any large fish, though there were some to be seen at the bottom of the pools; but by using a small rod and this very fine tackle, I did succeed in getting about ten pounds weight of the smaller fish, and though the largest was under one pound, I had many a good fight. The conditions made the fishing interesting, there was enough success to keep me at work, and if the result was not very remarkable, it was at any rate enough to give a feeling of having overcome difficulties, and saved what seemed at first a hopeless situation. It was very pretty fishing too, for one could see the gleam of the silver fish, even when they came short or took a fly under water. In similar conditions, but with a little breeze, I have found fresh run fish up to a pound and a half in weight rise freely. Fresh run sea trout are at all times exceedingly tender mouthed, and with small hooks one must expect to lose many of them even with the most careful handling.

Of all fish the sea trout fights the best in proportion to its size. Its strength when fresh run is greater than that of a brown trout of the same size, and being, as it often is, a stranger to the pool, or at best only a temporary visitor, it does not so often concentrate its

A narrow escape, by Joseph Crawhall

efforts upon getting to some known refuge, but rushes wildly from place to place. The fight of a sea trout is thus stronger than that of a brown trout and, if possible, even more active and full of quick turns. There is no fish with which one has to be so much on one's guard against being surprised, either by sudden rushes or by jumps in the air, and as far as the actual playing of a fish is concerned, for sheer enjoyment and rapidity of sensation, I prefer a good fresh run sea trout of three or four pounds in a river on a single-handed rod and fine tackle to anything else.

For this sort of fishing in a small river, I like to use a single-handed rod, but one that is very strong. One not only has more sport with the fish hooked on a rod like this, but one fishes more delicately, and can use finer gut than is safe with a double-handed rod; and finer gut makes a considerable difference in the number of fish hooked, except when the water is very much coloured. With a small rod an angler, who has nerve and patience, will land even salmon successfully on a casting line tapered to end with the finest undrawn gut, provided always that the water is free from obstructions, such as tree roots and weeds, and that the angler can follow the fish either along the bank or by wading.

Sir Edward Grey, *Fly Fishing*, 1907

On the Moidart

The Moidart river is a small one, and the house stood some way up it. In front of, and below, the house lay a small, shallow loch which in August and September was heavily stocked with salmon and sea-trout, and big fish could be seen jumping constantly.

By big I mean sea-trout of four to six pounds, salmon up to about seven – fine fish by west coast standards but small, of course, compared with the monsters of the eastern and northern coasts. Until it debouched into the loch the small river flowed deep and slow through treeless, marshy ground, and contained much weed. The edges of the loch itself were reedy, so that a boat was required to fish. Shortly after leaving the loch the river glided faster under a bridge as the ground began to fall away, and became largely inaccessible in woodland as it gathered speed. I caught the first big fish of my life at Moidart, and a great shock it was to all, especially the angler.

We had spent the day on a hill loch fly-fishing for brown trout. The hill lochs on the Moidart estate are reputed to be excellent, but this day was an angler's nightmare. For hours we sat in a boat in dead calm conditions. Fish rose round us and we cast despairingly over them, knowing it to be a pointless endeavour. It was overcast, dull, still, hot. Midges surrounded us, and fed. I had a migraine headache, arising from the stuffy air, or constipation, or just sheer frustration. At last we left and dragged ourselves wearily back to the lodge.

But I could never leave fishing alone in those days, when I was anywhere near it; I went off in the early evening alone, to flog the deep, slow, marshy stream above the loch. Conditions here were just as despairing as on the loch, though salmon and sea-trout are less predictable than brown trout. Until this time I had never caught any fish of more than three-quarter pound weight. I was about fourteen.

For my age I was quite a good, if impatient, fly-caster. But I remember exactly what happened before the great moment. It is a well-known curiosity that when something completely sudden and epochmaking happens to you, such as a car crash, memory instantly and vividly recalls the routine or humdrum events that preceded it; events that would normally have been forgotten absolutely and for ever within seconds. So it is that I can recall, even now, exactly how my cast fell on the water before the epochmaking event. I can clearly see the squiggles of it now; it fell in a horrible, feeble, curly tangle, the gut cast worst of all. There was clearly nothing to be done with it but forget it, haul it out before it sank too deep and try again.

Highland river, photograph by John Tarlton

As I hauled I found it had stuck on the bottom, possibly a log. I shouted to Miss Penn, who was fishing not very far below, that I had got stuck in a log. The log moved, but it still took seconds for the truth to penetrate – the impossible, incredible, heart-racing truth. This was a fish – and a big one.

Miss Penn came rushing up the bank, and I was grateful of company in my battle with such a monster. It is also immensely to her credit that she never attempted to seize the rod away from me as I muddled and bungled the desperate and vital challenge of landing a fish undreamed of. From her agitation it was plain what she was suffering, and what she would have liked to do, but unselfishness and iron will contained her so that all she did was to impart advice that was badly needed.

This fish was a beautiful clean sea-trout of three pounds weight. It was a monster to me then, and in a way I suppose it still is. It was much the biggest fish caught at Moidart that week, so its place of honour on a plate in the hall for all to see was not entirely undeserved. Everyone was more than polite and concealed their surprise at the happening – they would have been harder pressed to conceal it had they witnessed the piece of casting that led to the monster's downfall.

Lord Hardinge of Penshurst, *An Incompleat Angler*, 1976

Flies and their Use

Delightful Sport

My Lord, I will shew you the way to angle with a flye, which is a delightfull sport. The rod must be light and tender, if you can fit your self with a hasel of one piece, or of two pieces set together in the most convenient manner, light and gentle.

Set your line to your rod, for the uppermost part you may use your own discretion, for the lowermost part next your flye it must be of three or four haired links. If you can attain to angle with a line of one hair, two or three links one tyed to another next your hook, you shall have more rises and kill more fish. Be sure you do not overload your self with lengths of your line. Before you begin to angle make a triall, having the wind on your back, to see at what length you can cast your flye, that the flye light first into the water, and no longer, for if any of the line fall into the water before the flye, it is better uncast than thrown. Be sure you be casting alwayes down the stream with the wind behind you, and the Sun before you. It is a speciall point to have the Sun and moon before you, for the very motion of the rod drives all the pleasure from you, either by day or by night in all your anglings, both with worms and flyes, there must be a great care of that.

Let us begin to angle in March with the flye. If the weather prove windy or cloudy, there are severall kinds of Palmers that are good for that time. First, a black Palmer ribbed with silver. Secondly, a black Palmer ribbed with an orenge-tawny body. Thirdly, a black Palmer made all of black. Fourthly, a red Palmer ribbed with gold. Fifthly, a red palmer mixed with an orenge-tawny body of cruell. All these flyes must be made with hackles, and they will serve all the year long morning and evening, windy or cloudy.

Without these flyes you cannot make a dayes angling good. I have heard say that there is for every moneth in the year a flye for that moneth; but that is but talk, for there is but one monethly flye in the yeare, that is the May-flye. Then if the aire prove clear you must imitate the Hawthorn flye, which is all black and very small, the smaller the better. In May take the May flye, imitate that. Some make it with a shammy body, and ribbed with a black hair. Another way it is made with sandy hogs hair ribbed with black silk, and winged with Mallards feathers, according to the fancy of the angler, if he hath judgement. For first, when it comes out of the shell, the flye is somewhat whiter, then afterwards it growes browner, so there is judgement in that. There is another fly called the oak-flye that is a very good flye, which is made of orenge colour cruell and black, with a brown wing, imitate that. There is another flye made with the strain of a Peacocks feather, imitating the Flesh-flye, which is very good in a bright day. The Grassehopper which is green, imitate that. The smaller these flyes be made, and of indifferent

The fishing picnic, from an 18th century painting

small hooks, they are the better. These sorts which I have set down will serve all the year long, observing the times and seasons, if the angler have any judgement. Note the lightest of your flies for cloudy and dark, and the darkest of your flyes for the brightest dayes, and the rest for indifferent times; a mans own judgement with some experience must guide him: If he mean to kill fish he must alter his flyes according to these directions. Now of late I have found that hogs wooll of several colours makes good bodies, & the wooll of a red heifer makes a good body, and beares wooll makes a good body: there are many good furres that make good bodies: and now I work much of hogs wooll, for I finde it floateth best and procureth the best sport.

The naturall flye is sure angling, and will kill great store of trouts with much pleasure. As for the May flie you shall have him playing alwayes at the rivers side, especially against rain: the Oak flie is to be had on the but of an oak or an ash, from the beginning of May to the end of August; it is a brownish flie, and standeth alwaies with his head towards the root of the tree, very easie to be found: the small black fly is to be had on every hathorn tree after the buds be come forth: your grasse-hopper which is to be had in any medow of grass in June or July. With these flies you must angle with such a rod as you angle with the ground bait: the line must not be so long as the rod, drawing your flye as you find convenient in your angling! When you come to the deep waters that stand somewhat still, make your line two yards long or thereabouts, and dop or drop your flye behind a bush, which angling I have had good sport at; we call it dapping.

Thomas Barker, *Barker's Delight, or the Art of Angling*, 1659

Trout fishing, by Henry Alken

Aided by Hope

The lighter your fly and line descends on the water, the greater the chance of a bite; for, thereon depends much of the advantage the experienced Angler has over the novice, and which is only to be acquired by practice; and love of the art.

Never use more than one hook on your line at a time till you feel fully confident you can throw your line with one to any given distance or place: when you commence fishing any water, endeavour to keep the wind at your back, as it enables you to stand farther out of the Fish's sight; and you have the additional advantage of fishing both sides of the stream, if not very broad. In small streams, where the middle is shallow, you will always find a rippling on the surface, in the shallow part. When you cast in your bait, always take care to throw it on the opposite side, and draw it slowly to the rippling, letting it float down some distance; and if the Fish like your fly, they will certainly taste it; or, if you see a Fish rise in any part of the water you are fishing in, immediately throw your bait just above it, draw the fly gently over the spot where the fish rose, and, if done quickly and neatly, you will generally take the Fish.

Upon the curling surface let it glide,
With nat'ral motion from your hand supply'd;
Against the stream now gently let it play,
Now in the rapid eddy float away.

Having given a select list of artificial flies, and also enumerated several natural ones, accompanied with observations on their respective qualities and merits, how to cast or throw a fly, &c.; I shall finally take leave of the subject of fly-fishing, by recommending the young Angler, during his noviciate, to feel confident in pursuing the rules which I have laid down for his practice, and in the use of flies I have selected; and not to be easily put off his purpose by any person who may say that such a fly is unfit for this or that water, as some people are apt to speak hastily, from want of experience, or perhaps from local prejudice; for it will frequently happen that the fly which is the least praised will be found the most killing bait; there-fore learn to cast your fly skilfully, and expect sport in every stream you cast a bait in. Aided by hope and patience, and a favourable breeze, you will seldom fail taking a dish of Fish; unless, while the May-fly is on, there should be very heavy rains; if so, the flies are then beat down into the water, and the Trout glut themselves therewith, and will not take a bait for several days afterwards, notwithstanding

All arts and shapes the wily Angler tries,
To cloak his fraud, and tempt the finny prize.

Thomas Salter, *The Angler's Guide*, 1833

Grayling, by John Absolon

Plain Black Hackle

In June, or perhaps even in the latter end of May, a red quill becomes the more successful fly, and a medium size, neither large nor small, is the best. The trout have a tendency to prefer the smaller sizes, and when their appetite has become very delicate in hot summer weather the smallest possible size of red quill, not the smallest usually offered for sale in tackle shops, but one specially tied on the smallest hooks of all, is the most attractive.

This size may do very well with trout up to one pound or one pound and a half, but the hook is too small to hold strong fish of a large size. The fish lost after being hooked on these tiny flies far exceed in numbers those which are landed, and it is better to rise fewer fish with a medium-sized fly than to hook and scare the best ones without getting any of them. The same objection applies to imitations of that troublesome little insect the 'curse'.

The fourth kind of fly is a plain black hackle, tied with soft hackles, and on the same sized hook as the duns. It is always worth while to float this over an obstinate trout, and on many days at all seasons it has taken one or two brace of trout, which I am convinced I should not have succeeded in rising with the winged flies. There are occasions when the black hackle will take trout one after the other. I have a note of one evening, 16 June 1894, after the trout had taken a red quill well in the day-time. I had left off about two o'clock, and returned to the same meadow about six o'clock. The fish were rising again, but very quietly, and they persistently disregarded the same red quills that had been successful before. The black hackle was offered to them dry, and six fish were landed with it. One cannot of course expect the same success with this fly on every evening, but on many evenings, when the trout have been rising in their quiet evening way between six and eight o'clock, I have found the black hackle used dry better than any other fly.

I once had a remarkable experience with this fly. It was on 16 July 1892. There was very little rise in the morning; a few fish were seen, but as each one only rose about once in ten minutes fishing with the dry fly was very intermittent, and up till one o'clock nothing had been landed. It seemed that nothing more was to be done, and I sat gazing listlessly at the water. A fairly broad straight bit of river was before me, smooth in places, but with small ripples of stream here and there. The thoughts of other rivers and of

Angler and gillie on the Dee, photograph by John Tarlton

salmon fishing came into my mind, till at last in a state of sheer despair and idleness it occurred to me that I would try a wet fly, and in salmon-fishing phrase 'put it over' the piece of water before me. The black hackle, a very favourite north country fly, was chosen and used as a salmon fly, that is to say it was cast across and down the stream at an angle and kept moving gently, till the action of the stream brought it round to my own bank. The trout took it like salmon take a fly, sometimes under water, sometimes with a fair head and tail rise, sometimes with a plunge, but nearly always either when the fly was midway across the stream, or when it had come well round and was nearly straight below me; and the fish that rose took firm hold, hardly any being lost or only pricked. Now and then an isolated rise would be seen some way below me, and when the place was reached the fish nearly always came up well to the wet black hackle. At three o'clock I had six trout, and four more were added in the same way during the evening rise. The weather was not exceptional, being an ordinary fine summer's day with only a little breeze, some clouds, and intervals of sunlight. The part of the river in which this method had succeeded was not a hatch-hole or any exceptional place of that kind, but a clear, steady, even-flowing, well-fished stretch of the Itchen. It seemed that a great discovery had been made, and that the only difficulty was how to use it with moderation henceforth. Anglers are sanguine men, and are easily transported by unexpected success to heights of confidence; so they will, I trust, sympathise with my simplicity. I have on many occasions tried this fly in the same manner, in the same water, at the same time and also at different times of the season since, but never again has it succeeded to anything like the same extent. Perhaps in some seasons, when the yearly rainfall has ceased to be deficient, when this oppressive series of droughts has come to an end, and chalk streams are flowing strong, full, and clear above the weeds in midsummer, there may come another day such as 16 July 1892; but for the present I have ceased using the black hackle as a wet fly on chalk streams, not because it catches too many trout, but because it catches hardly any, and its record is classed in my mind with that of Single speech Hamilton, The Lost Chord, and other illustrations of amazing and isolated success.

Sir Edward Grey, *Fly Fishing*, 1907

Netting a fish, by George Barnet

For Making Flies

Get seals', moles', squirrels', and water-rats' furs also mohairs, – black, blue, and purple; also, white and violet; camlets, of every hue and colour; and fur from the neck and ears of hares; hogs' down, and bears' hair; also, hackle-feathers (hackles are long tender feathers, which hang from the head of a cock down his neck); get them of the following colours but not too large: red, dun, yellowish, white, perfect black.

Feathers to form the wings, &c. of flies, are got from the mallard and partridge, especially those red ones in the tail; feathers from a cock pheasant's breast and tail; the wings of the black bird, the brown-hen, the starling, the jay, the land rail, the thrush, the fieldfare, the swallow, and water-coot; the feathers from the crown of a plover, green and copper-coloured; peacock's and black-ostrich's herle and feathers from the heron's neck and wings. In most instances, where the mallard's feather is directed to be used, that from the starling's wing is generally preferred. You must also be provided with marking-silk, fine, strong, and of all colours; floss silk, gold and silver flatted wire or twist, a sharp knife, hooks of all sizes, shoe-maker's wax, a large needle, to raise your dubbing when flattened, and a pair of sharp-pointed scissors. A little portable vice is necessary to fix on the table, to which you may occasionally fasten your hook while dressing a fly.

Be particular in imitating the belly of the fly, as that part is most in the fish's sight, and make your wings always of an equal length, to insure your fly to swim true.

Most of those materials for fly-making may be purchased at the principal fishing-tackle shops in London. The articles for making artificial flies are prettily desribed by John Gay, in his *Poem on Rural Sports*, as follows:

To frame the little animal, provide
All the gay hues that wait on female pride:
Let nature guide thee. Sometimes, golden wire
The shining bellies of the fly require.
The peacock's plumes thy tackle must not fail,
Nor the dear purchase of the sable's tail;
Each gaudy bird some slender tribute brings,
And lends the growing insect proper wings:
Silks, of all colours, must their aid impart,
And every fur promote the fisher's art.
So the gay lady, with expensive care,
Borrows the pride of land, of sea, of air
Furs, pearls, and plumes the glittering thing displays
Dazzles our eyes, and easy hearts betrays.

Thomas Salter, *The Angler's Guide*, 1833

Coming to the net, by A. Rowland Knight

Flies and Salmon

The art of fly fishing for salmon bears no relation to any other form of angling with a fly. If it is akin to anything, it is to working a minnow rather than a fly, and the salmon angler must get all analogy with trout fishing out of his head.

The most essential points are skill in casting and knowledge of the river. In casting the object of the angler is to throw the fly above and beyond where he hopes the fish are lying, in such a manner that it may be brought by the stream moving in a lively and attractive way within sight of the fish, being gradually swept across to the angler's own bank. To do this successfully the angler must cast not only across but down the stream, and the more down stream the cast can be made the slower will be the pace at which the fly crosses the river, the greater will be the chance of the salmon seeing it, the less will be the chance of its seeing the line, and the more easy it will be for the angler to keep in touch with the fly during the whole time it is in the water. This is why it is so important to be able to throw a long line in salmon fishing, even in a comparatively narrow river: it is desirable not only to reach the whole of the likely water, but to cover it at a proper angle. If the cast is made directly across the stream, the line bags in the middle, and for the first half of the cast the fly has the appearance of a dead thing being towed down stream by a visible cord, instead of something alive being jerked by its own motion in the water. Two things especially should the angler bear in mind when actually casting and managing his fly: the first is that the salmon in fresh water has more curiosity than appetite, that he is not waiting for food, nor expecting it to come to him as he lies in the water. The fly must rouse the attention of the fish, and must do it attractively. It should have the appearance of something trying with difficulty to escape from him, and so perhaps arouse in him the passion of the chase, even when he has no appetite to be appealed to. This is why I think it is important that the fly should cross the stream slowly, but with a lively motion. The second point is that, as salmon lie either at the bottom of the river or not far from it, the fly should be well sunk in the water. To secure this in heavy water it is best not to jerk the fly violently, but to trust the stream to give the motion to the fly; and to use a long and heavy line. The most successful salmon angler, of whom I have ever had any knowledge, always fished with a big rod and a heavy and long line in the spring. I think his fish nearly always took under water, but he caught more than any one else on that river.

If we could watch salmon more in the water, as we can so often watch trout when feeding, we should learn much that would be of great practical advantage in angling, both in working the fly

The rise, by Norman Wilkinson

and in choosing size and pattern of fly for each day. After fishing for a few hours without a rise we get the impression that the salmon are not to be caught, and are taking no notice of the fly at all, but the latter is probably much less often correct than is supposed. Such opportunities as I have had of observing the behaviour of salmon at rest in the water lead me to think that the fish are continually taking notice of the fly and following it when we do not see them. I was once fishing with a friend on a beat of the Spean in June when the river was very low. We came to one of the best pools and found it so low and clear that we felt sure that it was not worth fishing, but when standing on a high rock above the pool we saw one good salmon of nearly twenty pounds' weight, and four or five small ones, lying together on a patch of smooth flat stones in the middle of the bed of the river. It was agreed that one of us should go down and fish the pool, while the other remained above to observe what happened. My friend went first, and as soon as the fly reached the fish, one of the smaller ones followed it without breaking the water. Time after time the fly was cast in the same place, and one or other of the smaller fish continually noticed it by some movement, or followed it to the bank, but there was no rise, nor was the fly actually touched. Then I went down and my friend reported from above. I succeeded in moving the big fish; he followed my fly two or three times, but none of the smaller fish made any movement. Then my friend tried again and moved more than one of the smaller fish, but without getting a visible rise from any of them or stirring the big fish. When my turn came again the smaller fish never moved, but the big fish followed the fly right round, and at last made a rise at it with a visible boil at the end of the cast, but without being touched by the hook. That was our nearest approach to hooking a fish, but we had enjoyed half-an-hour's very exciting sport. It was impossible for the person fishing to see these salmon while casting over them, and had either of us been alone, we should no doubt never have persevered long enough to get the one visible rise, which we did get, and should have asserted afterwards with perfect confidence that we had never stirred a fish. One curious point was, that though we changed patterns and sizes of flies, and interchanged them with each other, I could not move one of the smaller salmon, but only the big one, while my friend at different times moved every one of the smaller fish and never the big one. We had also on this day a very good illustration of the value of knowing a river. We had often fished this pool before, when it was in better order and the fish were not visible, and we now saw that the fish were lying in exactly that part of the pool where we had most often risen or hooked a fish. The reason seemed to be in these particularly comfortable looking flat stones, on which the salmon rested, but till we had once seen this, we had never realised the special virtue of that one spot in the whole pool.

Sir Edward Grey, *Fly Fishing*, 1907